CAREERS IN THE NEW ECONOMY™

CAREERS IN NUTRITION

LINDA BICKERSTAFF

THE ROSEN PUBLISHING GROUP INC.
NEW YORK

Published in 2005 by The Rosen Publishing Group, Inc.
29 East 21st Street, New York, NY 10010

Library of Congress Cataloging-in-Publication Data

Bickerstaff, Linda.
Careers in nutrition/by Linda Bickerstaff.—1st ed.
    p. cm.—(Careers in the new economy)
Includes bibliographical references.
ISBN 1-4042-0249-8 (library binding)
1. Nutrition—Vocational guidance.
I. Title. II. Series.
TX357.B58 2005
613.2'023—dc22

                                        2004014802

Manufactured in the United States of America

Photo Credits: Cover (background), pp. 4–5, 125, 127, 138, 139, 142 © Royalty Free Division/Comstock, Inc.; pp. 1, 3, 6, 114 © Royalty Free Division/PhotoDisc; p. 12 © Jose Luis Palaez, Inc.; pp. 30, 42, 55, 94 © AP World Wide Photos; p. 69 © Bob Krist/Corbis; p. 85 © Corbis; p. 106 © LWA-Stephen Welstead/Corbis; p. 107, excerpt from *Cool Careers for Dummies*, 2nd Edition, by Marty Nemko and Paul and Sarah Edwards, Wiley © 2001, reprinted with permission of Wiley Publishing Inc., a subsidiary of John Wiley & Sons, Inc.; p. 108, excerpt from *Mizzou* magazine, reprinted with permission of *Mizzou* magazine.

Designer: Nelson Sá; **Editor:** Wayne Anderson;
Photo Researcher: Nelson Sá

CONTENTS

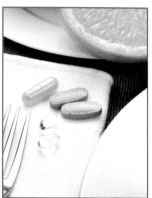

INTRODUCTION

140 160

The word "nutrition" has many definitions. *Webster's* dictionary defines nutrition as "the sum of the processes by which an animal or plant absorbs, or takes in and utilizes, food substances." Dorland's medical dictionary states, "Nutrition is the process of assimilating food." According to Carol Coles Caldwell, nutritionist, chef, and author of *Opportunities in Nutrition Careers*, nutrition is "the science of food, the nutrients and other substances therein, their action, interaction, and balance in relation to health and disease and the process by which humans ingest, digest, absorb, transport, utilize, and excrete food substances. In addition, nutrition must be concerned with social, economic, cultural, and psychological implications of food and eating."

Careers in nutrition, then, are careers dealing with food as it relates to our bodies and, more specifically, to our health and well-being. A career in nutrition could take you into space or to the training table of your favorite sports team. You might develop new, interesting, and nutritious foods as a food scientist. Perhaps you will help eliminate food shortages with genetically modified foods. Or, at the other extreme, perhaps you'll play a part in curbing America's present-day epidemic, obesity. There are careers in nutrition for people who like to cook, for those who like to take care of others, and for farmers, journalists, and sports enthusiasts. Perhaps there is a career in nutrition for you!

The job market for most nutrition careers is good and promises to expand through at least the next six to ten years. The expanding job market is being fueled by an increased awareness of the importance of good nutrition not only by the health-care community, but also by the corporate world and the general public. Traditional careers in nutrition are changing to incorporate new technologies. Nontraditional ideas within the nutrition professions are gaining credence and are leading to new career paths. An exploding world population demands expansive visions of ways to curb world hunger and malnutrition.

The goal of this book is to look at a sampling of present-day careers in nutrition that might be of interest to you as you start or continue your search for your niche in the working world. The future is bright for nutritionists. Job opportunities in nutrition are limited only by the imagination of those seeking them.

CHAPTER 1

THE AMERICAN DIETETIC ASSOCIATION

As early as 1902, the term "dietitian" was used for employees who were concerned with planning and preparing diets for hospitalized patients. Many of these people, mostly women, were graduates of training programs in home economics. Because of their interests and expertise, these women were soon supervising hospital food services and educating nurses and other health-care workers who were concerned about the role of diet in the care of their patients.

The onset of World War I in 1914 led to significant food shortages. Dietitians and home economists stepped forward to help the public meet this crisis. Modifying recipes for use in hospitals, teaching techniques of canning and other methods of food preservation, and demonstrating ways to prepare nutritious, meatless meals were just a few of the public services they performed.

BIRTH OF THE AMERICAN DIETETIC ASSOCIATION

Tracy Petrillo, in an article in the August 2002 issue of the *Journal of the American Dietetic Association*, tells of two pioneering women in the nutrition industry: Lenna Cooper, director of a training school in Battle Creek, Michigan, and Lulu Graves, supervisor of dietitians at Lakeside Hospital in Cleveland, Ohio. The two believed that it would be beneficial for dietitians, home economists, and others concerned with wartime food and nutrition issues, to meet for an exchange of ideas and information. They placed a notice in the October 1917 issue of *Modern Hospital*, inviting interested people to a seminar at the Lakeside Hospital in Cleveland from October 18 to 20, 1917. In spite of wartime travel restrictions and transportation difficulties, 100 professionals, representing twenty-one states and Canada, attended the conference. From this group emerged a new organization, which was named the American Dietetic Association (ADA). Lulu Graves was elected its first president.

GOALS AND FUNCTIONS OF THE ADA

Today the ADA is 70,000 members strong and is the largest organization of food and nutrition professionals in the world. The goal of the organization, however, remains the same as it was in 1917—to serve the public by promoting nutritional health in the United States and around the world.

REGISTRATION OF NUTRITION/DIETETIC PROFESSIONALS

One of the earliest steps the ADA took was to provide the public with the means of identifying those people who had the knowledge and skill to advise them about nutrition issues. The ADA established a ten-member Commission on

Dietetic Registration (CDR), which is responsible for setting the standards of education and knowledge for dietitians and dietetic technicians. The commission consists of seven registered dietitians (RD), one RD specialist, and one dietetic technician, registered (DTR) who are elected by the credentialed members of the ADA. The commission then appoints a public representative. Each member serves a three-year term. The ADA says, "CDR has sole and independent authority in all matters pertaining to certification, including but not limited to, standard setting, establishment of fees, finances, and administration." Its mission statement says, "CDR protects the public through credentialing processes of dietetics practitioners." CDR certification programs are accredited by the National Commission for Certifying Agencies, the accrediting arm of the National Organization for Competency Assurance.

The four credentials offered by the CDR are: Registered Dietitian; Dietetic Technician, Registered; Board Certified Specialist in Renal Nutrition (CSR); and Board Certified Specialist in Pediatric Nutrition (CSP). The mechanism for gaining these credentials will be covered in subsequent chapters of this book.

ACCREDITATION OF EDUCATIONAL PROGRAMS

In addition to providing the mechanism by which the public could identify qualified dietetic practitioners, the ADA also felt that it was important to provide high-quality educational programs to those who seek careers in nutrition as registered dietitians and dietetic technicians. The ADA established the Commission on Accreditation for Dietetics Education (CADE) to facilitate this goal. According to its Web site, "CADE is recognized by the Council on Higher Education Accreditation and the United States Department of Education as the accrediting agency for education programs that prepare dietetics professionals. Through the accreditation and approval of more than 600 undergraduate and graduate didactic, dietetic technician and supervised practice programs, CADE ensures that entry-level education meets quality standards."

FUNDING OF SCHOLARSHIPS, RESEARCH GRANTS, AND PUBLIC AWARENESS PROGRAMS

In 1966, in part to provide scholarships for many who wished to pursue careers in dietetics, the ADA established the American Dietetic Association Foundation. The goals of the foundation are not static and have changed through the years to meet perceived needs in worldwide nutrition. The foundation's current vision is to "be a leader in promoting and achieving healthy weight for children, helping to reduce the growing prevalence of childhood obesity." To do this, the foundation provides support for research, education, and public awareness programs. The ADA reports that in the last five years, the foundation has provided more than $1 million in educational support. In addition, it has provided funding for research projects being pursued by ADA members, especially projects dealing with childhood obesity. To increase public awareness of the present epidemic in childhood obesity, the foundation is funding the Healthy Weight for Kids Initiative.

DIETETIC PRACTICE GROUPS

Since its inception, the ADA's membership and its sphere of influence have grown significantly. In the ADA's early years, most of its members were clinical dietitians working in hospitals. Today, ADA members represent a range of practice areas and interests including public health, sports nutrition, medical nutrition therapy, diet counseling, food service management, education of other health-care professionals, and scientific research.

The ADA has established Dietetic Practice Groups (DPG) to serve as professional interest groups for its members. Members with similar interests may join together in one or more of the twenty-nine current DPGs to network, share ideas and information, and to provide support for each other. Example of DPGs include Diabetes Care and Education DPG, Dietetic Technicians in Practice DPG, Dietitians in Business and Communications DPG, Food and Culinary Professionals DPG, HIV/AIDS DPG, Sports, Cardiovascular and Wellness Nutritionists DPG, and Vegetarian Nutrition DPG.

OTHER FUNCTIONS OF THE ADA

The provision of reliable nutrition information to the public was one of the earliest goals of the ADA. Today it does this in various ways. The ADA's Web site, http://www.eatright.org, not only supplies information about the organization itself, but also has a wealth of nutrition information. It features approximately 3,000 pages of content from news releases and consumer tips to nutrition fact sheets and consumer FAQs (frequently asked questions). It also provides links to other Web sites that contain nutrition-related information.

In March of each year, the ADA sponsors National Nutrition Month. Members of the ADA provide school educational programs, write articles for newspapers and magazines, and attempt to raise public awareness of the benefits of good nutrition through other outreach programs.

The ADA publishes a professional journal, the *Journal of the American Dietetic Association*, to provide a forum for "original research, critical reviews and reports and authoritative commentary and information to nutrition and dietetics professionals throughout the world."

The ADA also works with local, state, federal, and international government officials to help develop policy issues dealing with nutrition. Members of the ADA provide expert advice to many government agencies, to businesses, and to educational institutions.

Although most members of the ADA are dietitians or dietetic technicians, membership in the ADA is available to almost anyone who has an interest in furthering health through good nutrition. As you continue to seek information about careers in nutrition, take a close look at the ADA. It can provide you with a wealth of information and help, and it may eventually be an organization you wish to join.

CHAPTER 2

CLINICAL DIETITIAN

Clinical dietitians are health-care professionals who are responsible for assessing the nutritional needs of patients and then developing plans to meet those needs. After developing the plan, a clinical dietitian either carries out the plan or supervises a dietetic technician in doing so. As a last step, the dietitian reevaluates patients to see if diet modification is necessary. The clinical dietitian is the food and nutrition expert and an essential part of the patient's health-care team. Dietitians work directly with a patient's physician, nurses, physical therapists, pharmacists, social workers, and others to ensure optimum care.

The role of the clinical dietitian reflects current trends in health care. Gone are the days of lengthy hospitalization for illnesses that are not life-threatening. For instance, less than than ten years ago, a patient with appendicitis could expect to be in the hospital for four to five days after an appendectomy. Today, a person with uncomplicated appendicitis is usually home within twenty-four hours of the operation. As a result of the trend toward shorter hospitalization, patients who are in hospitals for any length of time are usually very ill. Clinical dietitians helping to care for these patients face difficult challenges in assessing and implementing nutritional plans.

While one-third of clinical dietitians are still employed in hospitals and 12 percent in ambulatory care settings, the trend away from inpatient hospital care has led many to seek jobs in community and public health programs, extended care facilities, correctional institutions, and outpatient clinics.

INTERVIEW WITH
JOANNE LARSEN

Joanne Larsen maintains a Web site called "Ask the Dietitian" (http:// www.dietitian.com/ rds.html). On her site, she fields numerous questions on many topics related to nutrition. Here are a few of the questions she has been asked about clinical dietetics, and her answers.

Question: *I'm a junior in high school. I have always been interested in nutrition and am now considering*

Dietitians Recommend Clinical Dietetics As First Job

Most dietitians, regardless of their ultimate career choices, stress the importance of getting a firm foundation in clinical dietetics before considering other career opportunities. Nancy Clark, a sports nutritionist, says: "Although I had little interest in hospital dietetics [clinical dietetics], I saw the importance of developing a strong clinical background. Hence, I worked for two years in a hospital environment." She helped develop a page called "Career Corner" on the Sports, Cardiovascular, and Wellness Nutritionist Dietetic Practice Group (SCAN) Web site (http://www.scandpg.org). The first career tip given to dietetic students is, "Have a solid foundation in the practice of clinical nutrition. What you learn in your dietetics program is not equivalent to, nor a substitute for, clinical experience. On-the-job training is the critical period for the RD [registered dietician]; you will develop your own style of practice without your instructor's influence."

it as a career in the future. However, I don't know many dietitians and thought perhaps you could share with me the type of work a dietitian does, the advantages and disadvantages of your work.

Ms. Larsen: *If you are interested in food and how it nourishes the body or wellness and health, dietetics may be for you . . . The advantages are you work when people eat and are awake which is 6 AM to 7 PM, so there is no shift work like nursing or other health-care careers, but you may have to work weekends and holidays. It's exciting to see a person get better by changing what or when they eat. You don't have to know how to cook or even like cooking to become a dietitian.*

The disadvantages are that dietitians are 97% female who are not unionized and therefore, beginning salary can be under $30,000 per year for a new graduate . . . Most dietitians work with patients (clinical dietitians) or work with food service (administrative dietitians) either in hospitals, nursing homes or outpatient clinics. Some clinical dietitians work in private practice (counsel patients), perform nutrition research, consult with smaller health-care facilities or teach in colleges/universities . . . There are different areas of practice that dietitians work in/with such as public health, senior citizens, mental health, cancer, renal (kidney), children (pediatrics), diabetes, rehabilitation, sports and wellness, or school food service.

Question: *What kind of education and training did you receive? Which certifications and licenses?*

Ms. Larsen: *My bachelor's degree is in dietetics with a minor in chemistry from the University of Northern Colorado in Greeley. My master's degree is in nutrition with a minor in counseling and guidance from North Dakota State University in Fargo. I am registered with* *the American Dietetic Association and licensed in Minnesota. I did not do an internship but completed practical experience during graduate school instead. I worked one year as a student dietitian at the University of Illinois Research Hospital in Chicago between my bachelor's and master's degrees.*

Question: *What is your field of interest and in that field, which qualifications are [needed]?*

Ms. Larsen: *My passion has been clinical practice, but I also loved forming a nutritional support service (intensive care nutrition with oral or tube feedings or IV formulas) in a community hospital. So you would call me a generalist rather than specializing in say diabetes or pediatrics. I was the only clinical dietitian in a 173-bed hospital with an attached 125-bed long-term care facility (nursing home) so I worked with every type of patient and diet.*

Dietitian qualifications are a four-year degree in dietetics or nutrition with a nine-to-twelve-month internship or completion of a coordinated undergraduate program that combines classroom and clinical experience. When you become a registered dietitian, you have to take seventy-five credit hours [of continuing education classes] every five years. What that means is for every one hour spent in an educational program, you get one credit.

Question: *What work experiences and classes should I pursue while I am in school preparing to be a dietitian?*

Ms. Larsen: *I would first highly recommend that you talk to some dietitians who are doing what you think you would like to do. Then ask one of them to mentor you. Get a job in health care during college to see if you like the work. Don't spend four years of your life educating yourself for something you find you don't like or which* *doesn't meet your salary expectations. Your course work probably follows the educational guidelines from ADA for approved dietetic programs. In spite of this take outside courses in subjects that you would like to explore. The future definitely includes computer technology, complementary and alternative medicine— find out how it fits with health and wellness. Take some business and marketing courses as you will probably change careers at least eight times during your working life. Read newspapers, magazines and watch TV to see what aspect of nutrition the public is interested in, then educate yourself about it because they will seek you as the nutrition expert.*

FORECAST FOR THE FUTURE

In its 2004–2005 edition of the *Occupational Outlook Handbook* (OOH), the United States Department of Labor's Bureau of Labor Statistics (BLS) says that the outlook for employment of dietitians is "expected to grow about as fast as the average for all occupations through the year 2012 as a result of increasing emphasis on disease prevention through improved health habits." Fewer jobs may be available in hospitals. However, there will be more opportunities available in long-term care facilities, schools, and correctional institutions than there have been in the past. Establishing a base in clinical dietetics will be beneficial when looking for other opportunities in nutrition.

EDUCATION, TRAINING, AND OTHER QUALIFICATIONS

Clinical dietitians must meet the educational and professional requirements set forth by the ADA's Commission of Accreditation of Dietetics Education (CADE) for all dietitians. Most colleges offering programs in dietetics suggest that students pursue a college preparatory curriculum while in high school. This should include a strong emphasis on biology, chemistry, and mathematics. In addition, students are encouraged to gain computer skills, take at least an introductory course in nutrition or health education, and complete a course in psychology if it is available. Business courses, including accounting, will also be helpful.

TWO ROUTES TO REGISTRATION

There are two ways by which a person may become qualified to take the examination leading to registration as a dietitian.

The first of these involves attaining a baccalaureate degree from a college or university with a didactic program in dietetics (DPD) that has been accredited or approved by CADE. Carol Caldwell, in *Opportunities in Nutrition Careers*, points out that didactic programs require students to gain knowledge and demonstrate skills in eight focus areas: communications, physical and biological sciences, social sciences, research, food, nutrition, management, and health-care systems.

The didactic program in dietetics offered by the University of Florida in Gainesville is one of the DPD programs approved by CADE. Refer to Table 2-1 on the following pages for a sample schedule.

After successfully completing a CADE-accredited or -approved DPD program, a student must gain practical experience through a CADE-accredited dietetic internship before being eligible to take the national registration examination for dietetics. CADE-accredited internships are developed and overseen by a variety of organizations. There are currently 265 accredited dietetic internships.

The University of Maine's Department of Food Science and Human Nutrition offers a CADE-accredited dietetic

Table 2-1: Sample Schedule

University of Florida Didactic Program in Dietetics

Critical Tracking Criteria: Critical tracking courses are in boldface. A student should complete the boldface courses in the semester indicated with a 2.5 GPA to stay on track for this major.

Freshman Year   Credits

Semester 1—Fall

CHM 2045 General Chemistry (Lab)	3 (1)
Composition	3
Social Sciences	3
Humanities	3
Elective	4
Total Credits	17

Semester 2—Spring

CHM 2046 General Chemistry and Qualitative Analysis (Lab)	3 (1)
MAC 1147 Precalculus Algebra and Trigonometry	3
AEB 3103 or ECO 2013 or ECO 2023 or AEB 2014 Economics	3
Humanities	5–6
Total Credits	14–15

Sophomore Year   Credits

Semester 3—Fall

BSC 2010, 2010L Principles of Biology I (Lab)	3 (1)
PSY 2013 General Psychology	3
Humanities or Social Science	3
Elective	4
Total Credits	17

Semester 4—Spring

BSC 2011, 2010L Principles of Biology II (Lab)	3 (1)
MCB 2000/2000L Microbiology and Lab	3/1
STA 2023 Introduction to Statistics	3
HUN 2201 Principles of Human Nutrition	3
Total Credits	14

Critical Tracking Criteria:
All lower-division tracking courses must be completed by the end of semester 4, have a 2.00 University of Florida GPA, and have a 2.5 math/science GPA (in boldface courses).

Junior Year	Credits

Semester 5—Fall

CHM 2210 Organic Chemistry I	3
HSC 3032 Foundations of Health Science	3
FOS 3042 Introduction to Food Science	3
AEE 3414 Leadership Development in Agriculture	3
AEE 3030C Oral Communication or SPC 2600 Introduction to Speech	3
Total Credits	15

Semester 6—Spring

CHM 2211 and 2211L Organic Chemistry II (Lab)	3 (2)
DIE 3310 Community Nutrition	2
AEE 3033 Writing for Ag and Nutrition Resource	3
or English 2210 Technical Writing	
or MMC 2100	
HUN 3403 Nutrition Through the Life Cycle	2
PET 2350 Human Physiology	4
Total Credits	16

Senior Year	Credits

Semester 7—Fall

HUN 4445 Nutrition and Disease	2
DIE 4245C Medical Nutrition Therapy Applications	2
BCH 3025 Biochemistry or BCH 4024	4
DIE 4125 and DIE 4125L Food Systems Management (Lab)	3 (2)
DIE 4505 Dietetics Seminar	1
Elective	2
Total Credits	16

Semester 8—Spring

HUN 4446 Nutrition and Disease II	2
DIE 4246C Medical Nutrition Applications II	2
HUN 3221 Nutrition and Metabolism	3
AEB 3144 Agriculture Finance	3
FOS 4311 and FOS 4310L Food Chemistry	
and Experimental Foods (Lab)	3 (1)
DIE 4436 Nutrition Counseling and Communications	2
Total Credits	16

Balance of 120 credit hours necessary for graduation

internship. Unlike most dietetic internships, which are usually completed within a year, the University of Maine's internship requires two years for completion. According to the department, the internship is "combined with a graduate degree to prepare students to become Registered or Licensed Dietitians. The graduate degree obtained is either a master's or doctoral degree with a human nutrition or food science focus. Both thesis [research] and nonthesis options are available." Refer to Table 2-2 at right for a sample course sequence for the nonthesis option.

The second route by which a person may become qualified to take the registration examination is through an accredited coordinated program (CP). CADE has accredited fifty-one such programs in the United States. These are four-year programs that combine classroom work with supervised practical experience. The first two years of the program are almost exclusively devoted to classroom work. During the junior and senior years, students gain progressively more practical experience in various nutrition-related settings while continuing with advanced course work. Clinical experience in these programs is supervised by the college or university sponsoring the program. Successful graduates of these programs are eligible to take the registration examination for dieticians.

North Dakota State University's College of Human Development and Education offers a CADE-approved Coordinated Program in Dietetics (CPD). Refer to Table 2-3 on pages 22 and 23 for a sample curriculum of its program.

THE REGISTRATION EXAMINATION

The final step in becoming a registered dietitian (RD) is the successful completion of a national registration examination. This exam is administered by computer. According to the Commission on Dietetic Registration (CDR), which is

Table 2-2: Sample Course Sequence

University of Maine Dietetic Internship Program

Fall Semester I	Credits
FSN 650 Dietetic Internship Orientation I	2
FSN 571 Technical Presentations	1
EDS 521 Statistical Methods or equivalent	3
FSN 5-600 Level	3

Spring Semester I	
FSN 651 Dietetic Internship Orientation II	2
FSN 671 Advanced Graduate Seminar	1
FSN 5-600 Level	3
FSN 5-600 Level	3

Summer (May through August)	
FSN 681 Supervised Practice	1

Fall Semester II	
FSN 681 Supervised Practice	5
FSN 652 Dietetic Internship Evaluation	1

Spring Semester II	
FSN 5-600 Level	3
FSN 5-600 Level	3
FSN 5-600 Level	3

Supervised practice (6 semester credits) will be completed immediately following the first year of graduate studies from the end of May through December. In some instances, practice experiences may occur between the fall and spring semesters of the first year. Time allocations for supervised practice experiences are as follows:

Clinical Nutrition	19 weeks, 3 days
Food Service Management/Administrative Dietetics	6 weeks
Community Nutrition	4 weeks
Vacation	1 week, 2 days

Table 2-3: Sample Curriculum

North Dakota State University's College of Human Development and Education Coordinated Program in Dietetics

	Credits	
First Year	**Fall**	**Spring**
Anth. 111 Introduction to Anthropology	3	
Chem. 121, 121L General Chemistry I and Lab	4	
Chem. 122, 122L General Chemistry II and Lab		4
Econ. 201 Principles of Microeconomics		
or Econ. 202 Principles of Macroeconomics		3
Engl. 110, 120 College Composition I, II	3	3
HD&E 189 Skills for Academic Success	1	
HNES 141 Food Sanitation		1
Math 103 College Algebra		
or Math 104 Finite Mathematics	3	
Psyc. 111 Introduction to Psychology		
Humanities and Fine Arts Elective		3
Totals	14	17
Second Year		
Bioc. 260 Elements of Biochemistry		4
Biol. 202, 202L Introduction to		
Microbiology and Lab	3	
Biol. 221, 221L Human Anatomy		
and Physiology II and Lab		4
Chem. 204 Survey of Organic Chemistry	3	
Comm. 110 Fundamentals of Public Speaking		3
CSci 114 Microcomputer Packages		1
or CSci 116 Business Use of Computers		3–4
HNES 250 Nutrition Science	3	
HNES 251 Nutrition, Growth, and Development		3
HNES 261, 261L Food Selection and		
Preparation Principles and Lab	5	
Elective	2	
Totals	16	17–18

Credits

Third Year	Fall	Spring
Busn. 350 Foundations of Management		3
HD&E Professional Issues		1
HNES 340 Public Health Nutrition	3	
HNES 351 Metabolic Basis of Nutrition	4	
HNES 354, 354L Introduction to Medical Nutrition Therapy and Lab		4
HNES 361, 361L Food Production Management and Lab		5
Stat. 330 Introduction to Statistics	3	
Humanities and Fine Arts Elective	3	
Electives	4	
Totals	17	13

Fourth Year		
HNES 440 Nutrition Counseling Skills	3	
HNES 458, 458L Advanced Medical Nutrition Therapy and Lab	7	
HNES 460, 460L Food Service Systems and Lab	6	
HNES 480 Dietetics Practicum		12
Total Credits	16	12

Curriculum Totals 122

responsible for certification examinations, the registration examination for dietitians "is designed to evaluate a dietitian's ability to perform at entry level." The CDR provides the following information about the dietetic certification examination on its Web site (http://www.cdrnet.org):

- ACT, Inc., the testing agency for CDR, administers the exam at more than 200 approved test sites nationwide. These are located in universities and community colleges.
- Exams are administered at all sites Monday through Friday of each week and on Saturdays at some sites.
- The exam will vary in length. Each examinee will be given a minimum of 125 questions of which 100 will be scored. The maximum number of questions possible is 145, of which 120 will be scored.
- After taking an introductory tutorial to familiarize the examinee with the computer, each examinee will have 2.5 hours to complete the exam.
- A multiple-choice question format is used.
- Score reports will be distributed to examinees as they leave the test center. This report will include the examinee's scaled score and the scaled score required to pass the exam. The scaled score to pass the exam is 25 on a scale of 1 to 50.
- Unsuccessful examinees may retake the exam 45 days after their unsuccessful attempts.

Many candidates prepare for the examination by taking review classes. Many consult the *Registration Examination for Dietitians Handbook for Candidates*. As the handbook explains, the material covered by the exam is broken down into five "domains." The following table shows the percentage of questions assigned to each domain in 2002.

Domain	Percentage of Total
I. Food and Nutrition	15%
II. Clinical and Community Nutrition	40%
III. Education and Research	7%
IV. Food and Nutrition Systems	18%
V. Management	20%

The *Registration Examination for Dietitians Handbook for Candidates* is available upon request from the Commission on Dietetics Registration, 120 South Riverside Plaza, Suite 2000, Chicago, IL 60606-6995, (312) 899-0040. It provides sample questions that are illustrative of those found in the registration examination. Three of the sample questions are:

1. The first step in assuring a quality program for clinical dietetics practice is to:
   A. compare the productivity of the clinical staff to national means.
   B. monitor the quality of the documentation in the medical record.
   C. review current standards of practice.
   D. develop a tool to measure the amount of work done by the clinical dietitians.

2. Which of the following special supplemental nutrition programs requires that participants be at nutritional risk?
   A. Head Start Program
   B. Food Stamp Program
   C. Commodity Supplemental Food Program (CSFP)
   D. Special Supplemental Foods Program for Women, Infants, and Children (WIC)

3. Which of the following microorganisms are the primary cause of foodborne illness?
   A. Viruses

B. Bacteria

C. Protozoa

D. Parasites

Answer key: 1. C; 2. D; 3. B

CDR has recently released the seventh edition of its *Study Guide for the Registration Examination for Dietitians.* This includes a comprehensive study outline based on the 2002 examination content specifications, sources for each content area, practice examination, and study tips. The practice examination included in the study guide is provided on CD-ROM and paper. The questions are identical, although the CD-ROM version simulates the computerized registration examination format. These study guides may be purchased from the American Dietetic Association.

FURTHER REQUIREMENTS OF CLINICAL DIETETICS SUBSPECIALTIES

The role of the clinical dietitian is undergoing changes just as health care in general is changing. In order to meet the challenges of the complexities of clinical dietetics, several subspecialties have arisen. Many clinical dietitians find that becoming specialists in the nutritional needs of a specific group of people make them more valuable within the health-care team. Four of the subspecialties of clinical dietetics are certified nutrition support dieticians (CNSD, discussed in chapter 4), certified diabetes educators (CDE), and board-certified specialists in pediatric nutrition (CSP) and renal nutrition (CSR). Each requires the clinical dietitian to obtain further training beyond the basic skills of the clinical dietitian.

CNSDs may obtain a master's degree in nutrition and almost always work in a clinical or acute-care setting. Patients include trauma victims, patients with severe burns, patients with advanced cancers who are undergoing chemotherapy, or any of a number of other patients with life-threatening illnesses who need nutritional support (IV or tube feeding).

Certified specialists in pediatric nutrition (CSPs) are required to have specialized training in infant and child nutrition. This requires a dietician to meet established criteria and complete a specialty certification exam that simulates practice. These specialists may also work with pregnant women to improve prenatal nutrition and thus improve the health of the newborn child.

Certified specialists in renal nutrition (CSR) play a very significant role in the care of patients with kidney disease. Advanced study of food composition, body fluid composition, and the interaction between drugs and nutrients is necessary for clinical dietitians interested in this subspecialty. Being an educator is a large part of the job of a renal specialist.

A certified diabetic educator (CDE) must also have strong interests in educating patients. While not required, a CDE certification is very helpful for clinical dietitians dealing primarily with patients with diabetes. Diabetes is a very complicated disorder, and good diet control is essential to its successful treatment. The American Diabetes Association offers this optional certification for eligible health-care professionals.

The Commission on Dietetic Registration currently offers board certification as a specialist for registered dietitians in the areas of renal and pediatric nutrition. The CDR says, "Board certification is granted in recognition of an applicant's documented practice experience and successful completion of a clinical problem simulation examination in the specialty area." CDR provides information about specialty certification examinations on its Web site.

CERTIFICATION AND LICENSING

Forty-six states have laws that regulate dietitians or nutritionists through licensure, statutory certification, or registration. CDR says, "Dietetic practitioners are licensed by states to ensure that only qualified, trained professionals provide nutrition services or advice to individuals requiring or seeking nutrition care or information. Only state-licensed dietetic professionals can provide nutrition counseling. Nonlicensed practitioners may be subject to prosecution for practicing without a license. Refer to Table 2-4 on the following page for state and territory requirements for licensure and/or certification.

According to the Canadian Information Center for International Credentials, the profession of dietitian is regulated in Canada. Therefore, it is illegal to practice the profession or to use the title "dietitian" without being licensed as a full member in a provincial association.

SALARY AND BENEFITS

In 2002, the ADA's Dietetics Compensation and Benefits Survey reported that the median salary for registered dieticians employed in the profession for at least one year was $45,800. The BLS reports that the median annual income for clinical dietitians in 2002 was $40,000. Dietetic specialists earn more money as they have additional educational qualifications and more years of experience. Those involved in education, management, and consultation had median annual incomes of $54,200 in 2002.

Most clinical dietitians receive a good benefits package including paid holidays and vacations, health insurance, and some type of retirement benefit plan.

WORK ENVIRONMENT

Clinical dietitians have historically been employed in hospitals. The working environment is usually modern and clean, with good climate control. Long-term care facilities and

Table 2-4			
States and Territories Requiring Licensure			
Alabama	Iowa	Mississippi	Oklahoma
Alaska	Kansas	Montana	Pennsylvania
Arkansas	Kentucky	Nebraska	Puerto Rico
District of Columbia	Louisiana	New Hampshire	Rhode Island
Florida	Maine	New Mexico	South Dakota
Georgia	Maryland	North Carolina	Tennessee
Idaho	Massachusetts	North Dakota	West Virginia
Illinois	Minnesota	Ohio	
States Requiring Certification			
Connecticut	Missouri	Texas	Washington
Delaware	Nevada	Utah	Wisconsin
Hawaii	New York	Vermont	
Indiana	Oregon	Virginia	

The state of California requires registration only. Arizona, Colorado, South Carolina, and Wyoming have no regulations regarding dietitians.

correctional institutions may have less modern facilities, but the work environment is still comfortable. Certified nutrition support dieticians and pediatric care specialists may find themselves working in intensive care units, which can be crowded and noisy—a stressful work environment. Clinical dietitians may spend a good deal of time on their feet and be required to do a lot of walking throughout the day. The number of hours a clinical dietitian works each week depends on the organization for which he or she works. There may be need for some night, weekend, and holiday work, especially in the subspecialties.

CHAPTER 3

FOOD SERVICE MANAGER

The complexity of a food service manager's (FSM) job depends on many components, including the size of food service being managed, the nature of the food service, its location, and economic factors. An FSM, or administrative dietitian as dietitians in the food service industry are otherwise known, may direct all of the food services for a university, work for a chain of restaurants, or be the director of a public school feeding program. Most large restaurants, resorts, and casinos use contract food service companies that hire food service managers who work closely with executive chefs. FSMs may also work in hospitals, long-term care facilities, and other institutions.

While each food service has its own unique features, all food service managers have responsibilities in at least six different areas. The first area of concern is the development of the menu. This is done in close cooperation with the executive chef. It involves a knowledge and understanding of nutrition as well as the art of preparation and presentation of food. Some restaurants change their menus frequently while others offer a basic menu with daily specials featuring seasonal items. The FSM also prices menu items, estimates the amount of food needed to implement the menu, orders the food, schedules deliveries, and evaluates the quality of the food received. The manager constantly evaluates menu items to see which ones are popular, which are not, and which items are too expensive to prepare to justify keeping them on the menu. Food service managers in institutions, like correctional facilities for instance, may develop "set menus" that do not offer choices to the recipients. If particular items are consistently not eaten, these need to be removed from the menu to prevent wastage.

The FSM is also responsible for forecasting, which involves estimating quantities needed for ordering supplies such as paper goods, replacement glassware, and aprons. Major equipment items like microwave ovens, stoves, and dishwashers must be ordered, purchased, and kept in repair. The FSM oversees purchasing agents and others who may be involved in these duties.

Food service managers must have very good managerial skills because they are responsible for hiring, firing, training, scheduling, and supervising employees. This may be the most difficult part of the job because there is a constant shortage of food service workers. Many of those who work as servers in dining rooms or line cooks in fast-food restaurants are seasonal or part-time workers. This means that there is a constant turnover of personnel. Successful FSMs develop ongoing on-the-job training programs to train new workers in as short a time as possible. It may be necessary for the FSM to fill in if there are not enough workers for a particular shift.

The FSM supervises the kitchen, dining room, and tray line (in a hospital) to ensure the quality of food and service, and to make sure that all employees observe health and safety codes. This aspect of the job involves investigating customer complaints, dealing with the immediate problem, and making sure that the cause of the complaint, if justified, is dealt with so that it does not become an ongoing issue. If liquor is served, the FSM must make sure that liquor regulations are followed.

FSMs must also have business skills. Although the FSM may not actually do the work, he or she is responsible for seeing that records are maintained for all employees, including hours worked, wages, and salary deductions such as social security withholding and pension plan contributions. Inventory tracking, records of payment to suppliers, maintenance and repair records, and many other business concerns must also be done or supervised by the FSM. This necessitates knowledge of computers and the software programs pertinent to business. FSMs may also develop Web sites and maintain them for advertising purposes. In some parts of the country, restaurants post their menus and other information on their Web sites and even take reservations by e-mail.

INTERVIEW WITH NANCY WISE

Nancy Wise, administrator of operations at Oklahoma Christian Retirement Community (OCRC) in Edmond, Oklahoma, has many responsibilities, including overseeing the dietary department at OCRC. Here are highlights from an interview concerning the food service management responsibilities of her job.

Question: *What educational route did you take that led you to your present job?*

Ms. Wise: *I have a bachelor of science degree from Oklahoma State University in vocational home economics. This degree required course work and practical experience in nutrition, food preparation, and management with many education courses thrown in. I went to graduate school at the University* *of Oklahoma, majoring in education and geriatric studies, and received my nursing home administrator's license from OU.*

Question: *What do you do as the food service manager at OCRC?*

Ms. Wise: *Whatever it takes to get the job done. Among other things, I keep track of inventory; supervise others on the staff who do the ordering of food and supplies; help our chefs plan menus; hire, counsel, and fire dietary staff when necessary; and occasionally do a bit of cooking. Two maintenance men and I made stew and cornbread one evening when no one else from my staff could get to work because of a freak snowstorm.*

Question: *How do you handle special dietary needs of the residents at OCRC?*

Ms. Wise: *Many of the residents of our assisted living unit and health-care center do require special diets. OCRC contracts with a registered dietitian on a consulting basis. She evaluates the nutritional needs of our residents and recommends a dietary plan for each of them. I work closely with her to implement her plans. The trick is to take her recommendations and come up with food that not only meets the residents' dietary needs, but is tasty and affordable.*

Question: *Do you have any suggestions for students considering food service management as an occupation?*

Ms. Wise: *Food service management is a profession that requires expertise in many areas. You will probably find that you are more interested in some aspects of the job than others. Don't neglect those aspects that you don't like, because somewhere along the line they will be very important to you. Also keep up with new technology. When I started in the field, computers were huge boxes in the basements of universities accessible* *only to a few computer experts. I have had to educate myself in their use in the last few years because they help me to do the job more efficiently and effectively. Now I wonder how we could possibly get along without them. In this field you really have to be willing and able to do whatever it takes to get the job done.*

Forecast for the Future

The BLS reported that in 2002, there were about 386,000 food service managers in the United States. Of these, about one-third were self-employed. Employment opportunities will increase through at least 2012, with most new jobs arising in restaurants. Jobs in hospitals and correctional facilities will decline because many of these institutions are contracting with institutional food service companies rather than maintaining their own food service personnel. Long-term care facilities for the elderly are increasing in number as the population ages, so more jobs will be available in these facilities. There will also be a trend away from self-employed food service managers. Most restaurants are now affiliating with large national chains that provide salaried managers. Regardless of the employer, managers with college degrees will have the inside track for employment opportunities.

Education, Training, and Other Certification

A career as a food service manager can be approached from at least four educational routes. Registered dietitians with interests in business and management are finding food service management to be a good career choice. These administrative dietitians are required to fulfill the same educational requirements as other dietitians. In her book *Opportunities in Nutrition Careers*, Carol Coles Caldwell lists the following additional specific areas of study needed for a registered dietitian to qualify as an administrative dietitian in food service management:

1. **Principles of food systems management:** Provides an overall view of the management of food systems, including personnel involved in food preparation and service; equipment for operation; the purchasing of food and supplies; and the management of time and money.

2. **Quantity food purchasing and preparation:** Provides in-depth experience in menu planning, food preparation techniques, and cooking procedures to ensure quality food production.

3. **Development, utilization, and maintenance of physical resources:** Provides education in planning a food service facility, with exposure to equipment salespeople, consultants, engineers, and architects in developing the layout plan. Learns how to write equipment specifications and prepare cost estimates. Also learns equipment operation, sanitation, and preventive maintenance guidelines.

4. **Operations analysis:** Knowledge is gained in computer programming for use as a decision-making tool in food service for cost containment, food purchasing, stock maintenance, and as a carryover into clinical dietetics for modified diet menu planning and preparation.

Administrative dietitians are especially in demand for jobs in school feeding programs, college food service departments, and institutions like hospitals and long-term care facilities. They are also sought by institutional food service management companies because their backgrounds in dietetics provide needed expertise in nutrition. As restaurants, resorts, spas, and other hospitality facilities become more health conscious, administrative dietitians are going to be in even greater demand. Coupled with their training as registered dieticians, administrative dieticians would be well served to pursue specific training in food service management.

Many technical schools, colleges, and universities provide training in food service management. A bachelor's degree in restaurant and food service management provides a particularly strong preparation for a career as an FSM. More than 160 colleges and universities offer four-year programs in restaurant and hotel management or institutional food service management.

Johnson and Wales University (J & W) has a excellent program in food service management. The university has five campuses in the United States and a campus in Göteborg, Sweden. On its Web site, J & W University asserts that its bachelor of science degree in food service management prepares graduates for management challenges in the diverse, fast-paced, and rapidly changing food service industry. Its curriculum provides would-be food service professionals the opportunity to build on their leadership and management abilities, critical thinking skills, problem-solving techniques, strong financial analysis skills, and customer awareness. Refer to Table 3-1 on the following page for a sample curriculum.

Students in programs at J & W go to class four days per week, have the opportunity to obtain an associate's degree with two years of study, and progress on to a bachelor's degree with an additional two years of work. Through their Hospitality Cooperative Education Program (COOP), students who have completed their associate's degree training may be eligible for programs providing practical experience in food service management. If chosen for COOP, students earn an hourly wage and receive academic credit for the experience at host company sites in the United States and abroad. The university chooses the site where each student works. A few of the host sites included in this program are Trump Plaza Hotel and

Table 3-1: Sample Curriculum

J & W BS Degree in Food Service Management

First two years: Associate in Science Degree in Food Service Management

Third and Fourth Years

Major Courses	Credits
FM 3010 Beverage Service Management	4.5
FM 3070 Contemporary Issues in the Food Service Industry	4.5
FM 4061 Advanced Food Service Operations Management	4.5
HM 3050 Hospitality Strategic Marketing	4.5
HM 4060 Hospitality Management Seminar	4.5
Hospitality 3 courses selected from declared concentration	13.5
Hospitality 3 courses offered within the Hospitality College (electives)	13.5

Related Professional Studies	
AC 3025 Hospitality Financial Management and Lab	5.5
PD 0010 Career Management Capstone	1.0

General Studies	
EC 1001 Macroeconomics	4.5
EC 2002 Microeconomics	4.5
HI 2002 World History Since 1500	4.5
LD 3020 Creative Leadership	4.5
MT 2001 Statistics	4.5
PH 3040 Ethics of Business Leadership	4.5
PS 2001 General Psychology	4.5
SO 2001 Sociology	4.5
Total Credits	92
Four-Year Credit Total	194

Candidates for this degree are also required to
serve an internship at a J & W affiliated site.

Casino, Universal Studios, Hyatt, Hilton, Regal Hotels, MGM Grand, the Biltmore, and Walt Disney World.

Another exceptional program in food service management is offered by the Pennsylvania Culinary

Institute (PCI) in Pittsburgh, Pennsylvania. In 2002, PCI formed a partnership with the world-famous Le Cordon Bleu restaurant program, which was developed in South Australia in 1992. The Le Cordon Bleu management program provides theoretical and practical management, cuisine, and wine training. PCI claims that its "program meets the needs and desires of industry employers by spanning the gap between the 'front and back of the house' [dining room and kitchen] by including all aspects of managing restaurant facilities through practical, hands-on education viewed from the management perspective." Candidates can complete the sixteen-month program with an externship, selecting the site for training that will enhance their career path. Graduates of this program receive both an associate's degree and a diploma from Le Cordon Bleu.

The National Association of College and University Food Services, a trade organization for food service professionals, provides a full range of educational programs for those in the industry. One such program is a summer internship in food service management. This internship is a paid position. The salary is $1,600 for eight weeks of work with housing and meals provided. The total compensation package has an approximate $3,000 value. Applicants must achieve at least sophomore level in hotel, restaurant, and institutional management; food service administration; culinary arts; dietetics; or a related major. Students with related work experience and a strong interest in the field are also given consideration.

Program components vary with the sponsoring school. Between three and six weeks are spent learning the operation and its components from the service areas to the kitchen. The remaining two to four weeks are spent working with the professional staff honing management skills and working on projects. For further information on these internships, contact Holly Downey, chair of the Food

Service Management Internship Committee by e-mail at hkdowney@umich.edu, or by phone at (734) 763-5161.

A third route that can be taken for those interested in food service management is to become an executive chef. In an interview for the Cooking and Culinary School Directory at CookingSchools.com, Daniel Boulud, an executive chef and owner of Daniel, a four-star New York City restaurant, says, "Chefs cook, of course, but they also do a lot more; they need to hire, teach, manage, inspire, and encourage young chefs. The chef-owner has to do all that while keeping the department heads on track and giving direction to the business." These are the very duties required of a food service manager.

The Bureau of Labor Statistics' *Occupational Handbook* describes the fourth way to train as a food service manager: "Some restaurant and food service manager positions, particularly self-service and fast food, are filled by promoting experienced food and beverage preparation and service workers. Waiters, waitresses, chefs, and fast-food workers demonstrating potential for handling increased responsibility sometimes advance to assistant manager or management trainee jobs. Most restaurant chains and food service management companies have rigorous training programs for management positions. Through a combination of classroom and on-the-job training, trainees receive instruction and gain work experience in all aspects of the operations of a restaurant or institution food service facility. Training on use of the restaurant's computer system is increasingly important as well. After six months or a year, trainees receive their first permanent assignment as an assistant manager."

For those who want to work or are working in health-care–related facilities, another route to an FSM career is to obtain training as a dietary manager. Several colleges and universities offer independent study or distance learning programs, as well as more traditional associate degree programs, to help those who are working in the field gain the extra credentials to enhance their employability. An example of such a program is the Dietary Manager Independent Learning Program offered by Auburn University in Auburn, Alabama. According to the university, the program is designed for food service employees in the health-care field, particularly those in nursing home and hospital food service organizations.

The Dietary Managers Association developed a certification examination, which was first offered in 1985. It is part of the competency assurance program for dietary managers and was developed to recognize people qualified by training and experience to perform the responsibilities of a dietary manager. Only 11,000 dietary managers in the entire country have earned this prestigious credential. In 1996, a sanitation certification program (CFPP, for certified food protection professional) was added. The addition of this credential was very important to dietary managers because many state and local governments require food service managers to be certified in sanitation and food safety. Certified dietary managers now use the designation of CDM, CFPP after their signatures.

Another credential that may be important to the advancement of food service managers is the certified food service management professional (FMP) designation. Those that train on the job are especially eager to qualify as FMPs. FMP certification is awarded by the Educational Foundation of the National Restaurant Association after the candidate completes a series of courses that cover many topics in food service management and passes a rigorous written exam. Candidates are required to have three years of supervisory experience in restaurant or food service operation to be eligible to sit for the examination for FMP certification. If the candidate has an associate's or higher degree in business or hospitality, only two years supervisory experience is required. Candidates must also have earned a food protection manager certificate within a five-year period prior to applying.

SALARY AND OTHER BENEFITS

Salaries for food service managers vary with training and position. The BLS reports that in 2002, the median annual salary in this field was $35,790. The approximate range of salaries was between $21,760 and $67,490. According to Johnson and Wales University, regional managers of restaurant chains make as much as $80,000 per year, while a unit manager (a manager of a single restaurant) makes about $46,800 per year. Earnings for food service managers in institutions are considerably lower. In nursing and assisted living facilities, FSMs make median salaries of $33,910, while those in elementary and secondary school food services earn $31,210 per year. Salaries are lower because these jobs usually require only nine or ten months of work each year.

In addition to typical benefits, most salaried restaurant and food service managers receive free meals and the opportunity for additional training.

WORK ENVIRONMENT

Managers in restaurants work in dining rooms and kitchens, although they usually have an office where they do much of their work. Night and weekend work is common, although managers of institutional food services may have more conventional hours. The BLS says that it is common for food service managers to work fifty or more hours per week, seven days a week. It is not uncommon for them to work as many as fifteen hours per day. This is a high-pressure job requiring the ability to make good decisions quickly. It can also be physically demanding as it often involves much standing and walking and occasional heavy lifting.

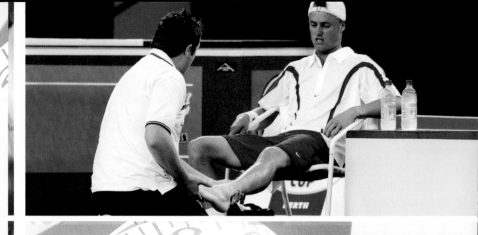

CHAPTER 4

SPORTS NUTRITIONIST

According to the National Association of Sports Nutrition (NASN), "The discipline of sports nutrition applies principles derived from current biochemical and physiological scientific knowledge for the purpose of promoting optimal health . . . Optimal health and the proper method of achieving this condition is urgently needed worldwide. The role of the licensed sport nutritionist is to facilitate this need."

Although sports nutritionists' day-to-day activities vary widely, there are two things they must consistently do in their profession. The first of these is to evaluate the client's nutritional needs to achieve optimal physiological function. Once the assessment has been made, the sports nutritionist then educates the client in nutrition and lifestyle modifications that will help him or her to reach the goal of optimal health, optimal performance in his or her chosen sport, and optimal body composition.

Barbara Sims-Bell writes in *Career Opportunities in the Food and Beverage Industry* that sports nutritionists have the goal of helping players achieve optimum health to improve athletic skills. They can provide guidance on every aspect of an athlete's diet, including high-energy snacks to eat on the road. They counsel athletes on which foods are easy to take to out-of-town games and how to stick to their diets when dining out. Sports nutritionists may even teach cooking classes to give athletes their independence from fast foods by showing them how to prepare simple, healthy, and inviting meals.

Sports nutritionists are employed by colleges and universities, health-care organizations that specialize in the care of athletes, professional sports teams, wellness clinics, fitness centers, and individual athletes. Some are self-employed as consultants in sports nutrition. Many sports nutritionists are also authors who educate the general public through magazine and newspaper articles and by compiling their knowledge into helpful and insightful books.

INTERVIEW WITH NANCY CLARK

When it comes to helping athletes achieve their goals by improving their nutrition, it helps if you are an accomplished athlete yourself. Bicyclist, marathoner, Himalayan trekker, and sports nutritionist Nancy Clark fits this description. Clark explains her work as a sports nutritionist in the following excerpts from an interview.

Question: *Would you briefly outline your educational background?*

Ms. Clark: *I completed my undergraduate degree at Simmons College in Boston, graduating with a BA degree in nutrition. Then, I completed my internship at Massachusetts General Hospital. Although I had little interest in hospital dietetics, I saw the importance of developing a strong clinical background. Hence, I worked for two years in a hospital environment. Next, I worked with the New England Dairy and Food Council* *as a nutrition education consultant. Concurrent with my personal interests in hiking, biking, and other outdoor sports activities, I recognized a professional interest in counseling sports-active people. I also recognized the need for further education in exercise physiology. Hence, I spent a year at Boston University's Sargent College of Applied Health Professions, where I graduated with a master's degree in nutrition, with a special focus on exercise physiology.*

Question: *What do you do as a sports nutritionist?*

Ms. Clark*: In terms of jobs, I was lucky to be in the right place at the right time. SportsMedicine Brookline, now called SportsMedicine Associates, hired me to develop a sports nutrition division. I'm pleased to be associated with this medical team of podiatrists [foot doctors] and orthopods [orthopedic surgeons]. In addition to individually counseling fitness exercisers and competitive athletes, I give talks to local high school and college teams and sports clubs, and present workshops for health professionals. I also write a monthly nutrition column that appears in almost 100 sports magazines and Web sites. I have written six books, the most recent of which are* Nancy Clark's Sports Nutrition Guidebook, *Third Edition, and* Nancy Clark's Food Guide for Marathoners: Tips for Everyday Champions.

Question: *What professional athletes have you counseled?*

Ms. Clark*: I have worked with members of the Boston Red Sox, the Boston Celtics, the New England Blizzard [women's professional basketball team] and also with many elite amateur and Olympic athletes from a variety of sports.*

Question: *Should all sports nutritionists be registered dietitians?*

Ms. Clark: *For quality control, all sports nutritionists should be RDs. Would you want to have a nurse who was* *not an RN? Many states have licensure, which means that only RDs can legally do nutrition counseling.*

Question: *Do you think dietitians should start working as sports nutritionists as soon as they are registered?*

Ms. Clark: *The majority of my clients are self-referred; they struggle with balancing food and exercise or present with complex nutritional issues. Hence, I believe sports nutrition is not an entry-level position. I also recommend getting a strong clinical background (i.e., working for two or more years in a clinical setting); the experience will be invaluable for an aspiring sports nutritionist who will be dealing with heart disease, cancer, pregnancy, diabetes, hypertension, and a myriad of other health conditions.*

FORECAST FOR THE FUTURE

Job opportunities for sports nutritionists should grow as well as or slightly faster than they have in the past. This growth will be driven by an increasing awareness of the importance of nutrition not only to trained athletes, but also to those who are beginning to get fit by increasing participation in exercise programs and activities. Sports nutritionists who are registered dietitians or nutritionists with advanced degrees in exercise physiology or other exercise sciences will have the best chance for employment and advancement.

SCAN TIPS

The ADA's Sports, Cardiovascular, and Wellness (SCAN) dietetic practice group provides information on sports nutrition, including tips for dietetic students or others interested in this profession, on its Web site (http://www.scandpg.org). A few of these are:

1. Be a role model—neither overweight nor underweight.

2. Gain experience by volunteering for sports and fitness groups.
3. Go to athletic events and clubs.
4. Do a personality check—sports nutritionists need to be able to generate confidence and enthusiasm. This requires you to be energetic and effervescent. If you aren't, you may want to look at another career choice.
5. Be a good listener.

EDUCATION, TRAINING, AND OTHER CREDENTIALS

Registered dietitians with a personal interest in sports are finding this field to be very rewarding. RD sports nutritionists must meet the same basic requirements as all other registered dietitians.

Some RDs obtain advanced degrees in exercise and sports science if they are interested in sports nutrition as a career. Texas Women's University (TWU) in Denton, Texas, offers a program leading to a master of science degree in exercise and sports nutrition. (Refer to Table 4-1 on the following page for a sample curriculum.) This program is suitable for registered dietitians who are interested in pursuing a career in sports nutrition. The prerequisites for this master's degree program are:

- A BS degree in kinesiology or nutrition, or its equivalent.

- A GPA of 3.0 or higher on a 4.0 scale on the last 60 hours of undergraduate course work with a major in either kinesiology or nutrition.

- Evidence of completing the Graduate Record Exam with a preferred minimum score of 400 on the quantitative portion, 500 on the verbal portion, and a combination score of at least 1,000.

- Official transcripts that provide evidence of prerequisite or the equivalent of undergraduate courses in exercise physiology, kinesiology, one additional upper division

Table 4-1: Sample Curriculum

Texas Women's University
MS Degree in Exercise and Sports Nutrition

Core Curriculum

KINS 5023 Methods of Research
KINS 5033 Applied Statistics
NFS 5313 Human Nutrition and Metabolism
NFS 5363 Human Nutrition and Disease
KINS 5573 Graded Exercise Testing
NFS/KINS 5583 Nutrition and Exercise
KINS 5613 Cardiovascular Response to Exercise
HS 5613 Healthy Lifestyles at the Worksite
NFS/KINS 5663 Body Composition and Weight Management
NFS/KINS 5681 Practicum in Exercise and Sports Nutrition
Total Hours in the Core = 30

In addition to the core courses, student must take from 7 to 9 hours of electives from the following list:

KINS 5553 Advanced Exercise Physiology
KINS 5563 Biophysiological Response During Exercise
KINS 5583 Hormonal Responses During Exercise
NFS 5333 Advanced Bionutrition
NSF 5384 Assessment of Human Nutrition
NSF 5453 Nutrition Education
NSF 6163 Nutritional Aspects of Obesity

For those students interested in pursuing research, teaching, academic positions, or a doctoral degree, a thesis is required.

NFS/KINS 5983 Thesis I
NFS/KINS 5993 Thesis II
Total Hours = 6

For students who wish to pursue an applied, practical program for clinical, community, or corporate positions, a thesis is not required, but a professional paper must be written.

NFS/KINS 5973 Professional Paper
Total Hours = 3

three-hour kinesiology course, human anatomy and physiology, biochemistry, elementary nutrition, advanced nutrition, and one additional upper division three-hour nutrition course.

• Two letters of recommendation and a one- to two-page statement of intent providing evidence of work and volunteer experience related to the intended field of study and goals.

One can, however, become a sports nutritionist without being a registered dietitian (although it may be difficult to find a job without an RD credential in most states). Most colleges and universities offer baccalaureate degrees in health and nutrition and in exercise physiology. With a background in either of these majors, additional course work in a master's degree program, like the one at TWU, qualifies one as a sports nutritionist. On the other hand, only four college or university programs now offer baccalaureate degrees in sports nutrition. Others are being developed. One such program was approved in 2000, at Mansfield University in Mansfield, Pennsylvania. (Refer to Table 4-2 on pages 50 and 51 for a sample schedule.) The objective of this program as listed on Mansfield University's Web site (http://www. mnsfld.edu) is that graduates of the fitness and sports nutrition program should be able to:

• Utilize theories from the natural sciences, social sciences, exercise physiology, and nutrition to assist individuals at all stages of life to attain and maintain optimal physical fitness and nutrition status.

• Demonstrate the ability to assess, implement, and evaluate the fitness and nutritional needs of well individuals and groups.

• Recommend the proper nutrition and exercise protocol for those who wish to develop and maintain healthy lifestyles.

- In conjunction with health-care professionals, assess the fitness and nutritional needs of individuals with chronic illnesses.

- Collaborate with health professionals and consumers to support changes in overall health behaviors for the welfare of society.

- Demonstrate accountable and ethical behavior in compliance with established standards as nutrition recommendations are made for athletes of all ages and fitness levels.

The program allows graduates to take jobs immediately after graduation in corporate wellness centers; fitness centers; professional, collegiate, or amateur sports teams; sports training camps; hospitals; health clubs; or sports clinics.

Certification examinations are not required in sports nutrition. However, the American Academy of Sports Dietitians and Nutritionists (AASDN) has recently developed a Graduate Sports Nutrition Certification program. The academy is a nonprofit organization that claims to be the first national organization to recognize the achievements of licensed dietitians and nutritionists with extensive experience and education in a fitness related field. According to its Web site, the AASDN is "dedicated to establishing and maintaining high standards for the promotion of accurate, scientific, nutrition information as it relates to sports and wellness programming." Academy membership requirements are:

- Licensure as a dietitian/nutritionist by the ADA (or an equivalent state license as a registered dietitian/nutritionist) or a graduate degree from an accredited college or university in human nutrition, nutrition education, food and nutrition, or public health nutrition, or in an equivalent major course of study, with proof of 900

Table 4-2: Sample Schedule

Mansfield University
Bachelor's Degree in Sports Nutrition

	Credits
First Semester	
CHM 101 Introduction to Chemistry	4
COM 101 Oral Communications	3
DIT 211 Introduction to Nutrition	3
PSY 101 Introduction to General Psychology	3
Health or HPE Electives	2
Second Semester	
CHM 102 Organic and Biochemistry	4
ENG 112 Composition	3
DIT 3056 Principles of Food Science	3
BUS 130 Introduction to Business and Management	3
Fine Arts Elective	3
Third Semester	
BSC 121 Human Anatomy and Physiology I	4
DIT 314 Lifecycle Nutrition	3
MA 125 Introduction to Statistics	3
Humanities, Social Science, Language	3
Elective	3
Fourth Semester	
BSC 122 Human Anatomy and Physiology II	4
DIT 316 Community Nutrition	3
Humanities, Social Science, Language	3
General Education Elective	3
Elective	3

Credits

Fifth Semester

CHM 201 Biochemistry	4
ENG 312 Composition II	3
HPE Kinesiology	3
Humanities, Social Science, Language	3
Elective	1

Sixth Semester

DIT 330 Sports Nutrition	3
DIT 325 Nutritional Education, Counseling	3
HPE 370 Physiology of Exercise	3
Humanities, Social Science, Language	3
HPE Elective	1

Seventh Semester

DIT 417 Advanced Nutrition	3
Math Elective	3
General Education Elective	3
General Education Elective	6

Eighth Semester

DIT 420 Nutrition Research	3
Humanities, Social Science, Language	3
DIT Electives	3
General Education Elective	3
Electives	3
Total Credits Required	120

hours of professional experience associated with the earned degree.

- Certification in a nationally recognized fitness organization (ACSM, ACE, AFAA, NASM, NATA, NSCA) or a bachelor's, master's, or doctoral degree from an accredited college or university that includes a major course of study in exercise physiology, or its equivalent, with not less than a combined 200 hours of exercise science. Proof of 900 hours professional experience associated with the earned degree.
- Proof of one year of full-time professional experience in a sports nutrition position.
- Three professional references.

AASDN's Graduate Sports Nutrition Certification program is offered to registered dietitians and licensed nutritionists. The certification program requires participation in eight two-day educational modules. Candidates receive sixteen to eighteen credit hours for each program. These modules include: 1) sports-related biochemistry and working with the exercising public; 2) exercise prescription; 3) regulations—drugs, supplements, herbal medications, ergogenic aids, and ethics in science; 4) working with varied population; 5) working with the aging population; 6) making it a business; 7) making it a business concluded; 8) working with athletes—health assessment and metabolic techniques.

In addition to successful completion of these modules, candidates must show proof of working with at least twenty clients and at least sixty hours of experience. They must also be certified in a nationally recognized fitness organization or possess a bachelor's, master's, or doctoral degree from an accredited college or university with a major in exercise physiology or its equivalent. Students must also complete a presentation on a nutrition-related topic and pass a comprehensive examination.

PROFILE: DAN BENARDOT

Dr. Dan Benardot is a sports nutritionist and an associate professor of nutrition, kinesiology, and health at Georgia State University. He is also codirector of the Laboratory of Elite Athlete Performance at GSU. In 2000, he worked with track and field athletes and gymnasts at the Summer Olympic Games in Sydney, Australia. There, he continually reminded the athletes of the importance of sticking to routines. He said, "It is important for the athletes to remember what got them there [to the Olympics]. Routine is very critical, and that includes food," as quoted in "Fueling Olympic Fires," an article by Janet Keeler in the September 13, 2000, issue of the *St. Petersburg Times*.

According to Dr. Benardot, athletes in different sports approach their diets differently. Sprinters, short-distance swimmers, and gymnasts need to guard against drinking too much fluid before they compete. Too much hydration causes muscle stiffness, which is a detriment in events lasting a short time. Distance runners, on the other hand, must "hyperhydrate" shortly before competing.

Dr. Benardot also spoke about how athletes are often superstitious about food. Many believe that particular foods make them more successful in their athletic events. He gave the example of an athlete who has a superstition about tuna sandwiches. If the athlete cannot get a tuna sandwich before competing, he may not do as well as he would have done had he eaten a tuna sandwich just before competing. Dr. Benardot encourages athletes to bring specific foods with them if that gives them peace of mind. He says, "Invariably they will find foods they like, but if you can give them a sense of security they perform better."

SALARY AND BENEFITS

Barbara Sims-Bell says that salaries for sports nutritionists range from $25,000 per year to about $40,000 per year.

Most RDs who specialize in sports nutrition have master's degrees in nutrition and/or sports sciences. These additional credentials are usually reflected in higher salaries of $50,000 or more per year. Sports nutrition consultants may make considerably more than salaried sport nutritionists, but they must also pay many of their own expenses, which tends to equalize income. Most salaried sports nutritionists receive a full range of benefits, including paid holidays and vacations as well as pension plan options and paid health insurance. Self-employed consultants do not receive these benefits, but they can purchase them for themselves.

WORK ENVIRONMENT

Sports nutritionists working in educational institutions will do most of their work in well-lit, pleasant classrooms or offices. They may also spend time at training tables, in demonstration kitchens, or in gymnasiums. Those who work in wellness centers, fitness centers, or health clubs may work in a gymlike atmosphere and very posh surroundings. Work hours are usually regular and scheduled with little, if any, night or holiday work. Consultants who present seminars may, however, work at night and on weekends, when most seminars are given. Sports nutritionists who work for sports teams may travel with them and therefore have both irregular hours and variable work conditions. Sports nutritionists, for the most part, practice what they preach and are themselves athletes. This is helpful because being in good physical condition is a must for this active occupation.

CHAPTER 5

NUTRITION SUPPORT DIETITIAN/NUTRITION SUPPORT PHARMACIST

All careers in nutrition are important. Those of certified nutrition support dietitian (CNSD) and board-certified nutrition support pharmacist (BCNSP), however, often involve matters of life or death. Perhaps that sounds a bit dramatic, but to those who cannot eat or who have medical conditions that make it impossible for them to use their digestive tracts in the normal manner, these professionals can not only sustain life but make that life worth living.

The American Society of Parenteral and Enteral Nutrition (ASPEN) has published an article entitled "What Is PEN," which states: "Sometimes a person cannot eat any or enough food because of an illness. The stomach or bowel may not be working quite right, or a person may have had surgery to remove part or all of these organs. Under those conditions, nutrition must be supplied in a different way." That way is with either parenteral or enteral nutrition, or sometimes both. Certified nutrition support dietitians and pharmacists work with patients who require the use of parenteral and enteral nutrition (PEN).

Parenteral nutrition is a liquid that contains all of the nutrients a person needs. It is made in such a way that it can be injected directly into a person's blood through a needle or catheter, which is placed into a large vein. It is sometimes called hyperalimentation or total parenteral nutrition (TPN). It is used in patients who cannot rely on their digestive tracts to digest and absorb enough nutrients to sustain life.

Enteral nutrition is also a liquid. However, it is much thicker and cannot be fed through a vein. Another name for enteral nutrition is tube feeding (TF). People whose intestines can absorb food but who cannot eat benefit from enteral nutrition. Patients who have been involved in car wrecks or other accidents and are unconscious, for instance, are not able to eat. If they do not have any absorption problems, feeding tubes can be placed into their stomach or intestines to deliver nutrients. A patient who has had a stroke, or a baby who has been born with abnormalities of its esophagus or stomach are other examples of patients for whom enteral nutrition is critical.

Duties of nutrition support professionals range from actually formulating the TPN/TF to helping individuals or their caregivers learn to administer their feedings at home. Nutrition support personnel frequently work as a team, with each member of the team contributing special talents toward giving the patient the very best care.

FORECAST FOR THE FUTURE

The demand for nutrition support professionals, and especially for nutrition support teams, has grown steadily in recent years and will continue to expand in the future. Patients who are in hospitals for long periods are frequently those who need the services of nutrition support personnel. As a result of the increasing trend toward shorter hospitalization, more nutrition support professionals are needed to help with home care and the education of patients and caregivers who are trying to care for themselves or their loved ones at home. This is a growth field and one in which innovations are constantly expanding the scope of the job.

EDUCATION, TRAINING, AND OTHER CERTIFICATION

Registered dietitians comprise a significant number of people working with TPN/TF patients, especially with those receiving enteral nutrition. RDs in this field must meet the basic requirements for registration as do all other RDs.

Dietitians who specialize in nutrition support are usually clinical dietitians with an interest in critical care dietetics. While they receive on-the-job training with both TPN and enteral nutrition in the intensive care unit, they usually take additional course work leading to a master's degree in nutrition. An example of the curriculum of a program leading to a master of science degree in nutrition is found in the 2003–2004 Graduate School Bulletin of the University of Massachusetts at Amherst. This program requires that candidates have a bachelor's degree in nutrition or a related field such as biochemistry, biology, exercise science, food science, physiology, or public health. The focus of the program can be either on nutrition sciences or on community nutrition. Both thesis and nonthesis options are available. Refer to Table 5-1 on the following page for degree requirements.

Dietitians may elect to seek certification in nutrition support after working for two years in the field. The National Board of Nutrition Support Certification, Inc.,

Table 5-1: Degree Requirements

University of Massachusetts at Amherst
Master of Science Degree in Nutrition

The thesis option requires a minimum of 32 graduate credits and the non-thesis option a minimum of 36 credits.

Nutrition Core—These courses must be taken by those who do not have a BS degree in nutrition. Graduate credits are given for courses numbered above 500.

Nutritn 352 Life Cycle Nutrition
Nutritn 572 Community Nutrition
Nutritn 577 Nutritional Problems in the U.S.
Nutritn 579 Nutrition and Disease
Nutritn 581 Clinical Dietetics Practice
ExerSci 597B Energy Metabolism or Nutritn 430 Nutrition and Metabolism

Advanced Nutrition Core (11 credits)—These courses must be taken by all enrolled in the MS program.
Nutritn 697A Special Topics in Nutrition, Metabolism, and Chronic Disease
Nutritn 731 Nutritional Assessment
Nutritn 793/4 Seminar (2 semesters, 2 credits)
Biost&Ep Introductory Biostatistics

Nutrition Concentration (6 credits)—Choose either the nutrition sciences or the community nutrition concentration
Nutrition Sciences
  Nutritn 714 Advanced Nutrition Vitamins
  Nutritn 715 Advanced Nutrition Minerals
Community Nutrition
  Nutritn 697B Special Topics Public Health Nutrition
  Nutritn 597 Nutrition Counseling

Electives (6 credits)
Nutrition Sciences—Two courses with at least one from outside the department
Community Nutrition
Biost&Ep Principles of Epidemiology
And one course from outside the department

Culminating Experience—Choose from thesis or nonthesis options
Thesis Option (9–13 credits)
  Biost&Ep 640 Intermediate Biostatistics
  Nutritn 699 MS thesis (6–10 credits)
Nonthesis Option (13 credits)
  6 credits of course work at the 500 level or above, within or outside the department, plus:
  Nutrition Science
  Nutritn 696 Research Problems (6 credits) and one additional seminar, special topics course of journal club (1 credit)

Community Nutrition
Nutritn 696 Research Problems (6 credits)
Nutritn 698 Practicum (3 credits)

(NBNSC) is an independent board established in 1984 by ASPEN to develop and administer certification exams. It endorses the concept of voluntary, periodic certification by examination for nutrition support dietitians. Board certification for an NSD is highly valued and provides formal recognition of basic nutrition support knowledge. NBNSC says that the objective of offering certification in the field of nutrition support is "to promote enhanced delivery of safe and effective care through the certification of qualified nutrition support dietitians." Board certification is a degree-independent form of quality assurance that the practitioner possesses a defined set of knowledge and skills.

The certification examination is a computer-based examination given at more than 700 sites throughout the United States by the Professional Testing Corporation. It can be taken Monday through Saturday over a two-week testing period. It may be taken as often as necessary for successful completion. Twenty-seven percent of exam questions cover nutrition assessment and reassessment, 40 percent deal with therapeutic plans and the implementation of these plans, and 27 percent are concerned with patient monitoring and evaluation. The remaining 6 percent deal with professional issues. The following are sample questions from the examination.

1. During parenteral nutrition, the infusion of large amounts of dextrose increases electrolyte requirements for
    1. Sodium and potassium
    2. Sodium and phosphorous
    3. Potassium and chloride
    4. Potassium and phosphorous

2. Indirect calorimetry provides a measure of
    1. Basal metabolic rate
    2. Past 24-hour dietary intake

3. Energy expenditure
4. Calories needed for weight gain

3. An 85-year-old woman receiving tube feeding because of dysphagia develops increased stooling and has a temperature of 38.3 degrees [Celsius]. Which of the following should be done?
1. Obtain stool cultures
2. Decrease water flushes
3. Begin diphenoxylate and atropine
4. Change to fluid-restricted tube-feeding formula

Answer key: 1. 4; 2. 3; 3. 1

After successfully completing the exam, candidates receive a certificate and are entitled to use "CNSD" after their names. Certification must be renewed by examination every five years.

Many patients who need TPN/TF have chronic problems that will not be resolved quickly. In order to try to normalize their lives, and also to control costs, it is beneficial for these patients to get their TPN/TF at home. Jill Place, who has served on the editorial board of ASPEN, says that registered dietitians are especially important to nutrition support teams dealing with home PEN. In addition to their other functions on the home PEN team, they serve as the primary educators for the patient and/or the patient's caregivers. This requires that dietitians in the field have especially good communication skills.

In 1988, the ADA declared in a position statement that "the registered dietitian [should] assume a key role in the medical nutrition therapy for patients receiving home parenteral and enteral nutrition support to provide appropriate and cost-effective nutrition care." This statement was reaffirmed in 1997. In addition to the other duties assigned to the dietitian on the PEN team, the dietitian is also the person who coordinates the patient's transition from parenteral and enteral therapy to an oral diet.

NUTRITION SUPPORT PHARMACISTS

Clinical pharmacists are also important members of the nutrition support team. Pharmacists deal mainly with TPN. A pharmacist is a health professional who specializes in the science of drugs or medications. Pharmacy is the third-largest health profession in the United States and is one of the most financially rewarding careers in health care. In order to qualify for acceptance into a pharmacy program, high school students should take courses in biology, chemistry, physics, and math. Good written and verbal skills are necessary, so high school students should have a strong foundation in English. Personal qualities that are assessed in those applying for pharmacy school are good judgment, dependability, and attention to detail.

The doctor of pharmacy (Pharm.D.) degree program requires students to take at least two years of undergraduate coursework. The requirements for what must be included in these two years varies from one school of pharmacy to the other, but all emphasize chemistry courses. Most students accepted to a college of pharmacy have three or more years of undergraduate college experience. About half of all schools of pharmacy require applicants to submit scores from a standardized Pharmacy College Admission Test (PCAT).

Some pharmacy programs accept students directly from high school for the two years of prepharmacy courses. It takes a minimum of three years in a school of pharmacy to complete the pharmacy curriculum leading to a bachelor of pharmacy degree. However, this degree is offered in few schools of pharmacy today. Most programs require two to three years of prepharmacy and four years of pharmacy leading directly to the Pharm.D. degree. A pharmacy internship or supervised practical experience is required before a pharmacist may apply for licensure.

The practice of pharmacy within each state is regulated by the laws of the state. Pharmacists are licensed by the State Board of Pharmacy. Requirements vary somewhat from state to state, but in general, to be licensed, a pharmacist must be a graduate of an accredited college of pharmacy and have completed a residency or internship program to acquire hands-on patient care experience. He or she must also pass a rigorous exam called the National Association of Boards of Pharmacy Licensing Examination (NABPLEX). The state of California does not recognize NABPLEX, but it administers its own licensure examination.

The NABPLEX is a computer-adaptive test that assesses a candidate's ability to apply knowledge gained in pharmacy school to practical situations. It is made up of 185 five-option multiple-choice questions. Groups of questions are usually preceded by a patient profile or scenario on which the questions are based. The exam must be completed within four hours and fifteen minutes. It is given Monday through Friday at Prometric Testing Centers throughout the United States. A second exam, called the Pharmacy Jurisprudence Examination, is required by forty-five states. It is also administered in Prometric Testing Centers. It is a computer-adaptive exam consisting of ninety five-option multiple-choice questions and must be completed within two hours. Most states also require pharmacists to pass a drug law examination before licensing is completed.

According to Joanne Whitney of the School of Pharmacy at the University of California, San Francisco: "TPN training is included in a basic pharmacy degree, but it is a very complicated field and there is a great deal of on-the-job training and special courses [for those working with TPN]." The American Pharmacy Association (APA), in recognition of the complexity of nutrition support, added the category of nutrition support pharmacist to its list of pharmacy specialties. The APA established an independent Board of Pharmacy Specialties to develop, administer, and score certification examinations in areas requiring specialized training for pharmacists. Nutrition support pharmacist is one of five recognized pharmacy specialties, each with its own certification examination. As of January 2003, there were 391 board-certified nutrition support pharmacists in the United States.

The 2004 *Candidate's Guide to Specialty Certification*, published by the Board of Pharmaceutical Specialties, says, "Nutrition support pharmacy addresses the care of patients who receive specialized nutrition support, including parenteral and enteral nutrition. The nutrition support pharmacist has responsibility for promoting maintenance and/or restoration of optimal nutrition status, designing and modifying treatment according to the needs of the patient. The nutrition support pharmacist has responsibility for direct patient care and often functions as a member of a multidisciplinary nutrition support team." The handbook lists the following eligibility requirements for certification in the specialty:

- Graduation from a pharmacy program accredited by the American Council on Pharmaceutical Education or an alternative educational program accepted by BPS.

- Current active license to practice pharmacy.

- Completion of three years' practice experience with substantial time spent in nutrition support pharmacy activities; or completion of a specialty residency in nutrition support pharmacy practice plus one additional year of practice; or completion of a nutrition support fellowship plus one additional year of practice experience; or completion of BOTH a specialty residency in nutrition support pharmacy and a nutrition support fellowship.

- Achieving a passing score on the Nutrition Support Pharmacy Specialty Certification Examination.

The certification examination is given on the first Saturday of October at twenty testing sites throughout the United States. The exam is made up of 200 multiple-choice questions meant to sample the knowledge and skills required to perform the tasks in nutrition support pharmacy. The content of the examination is broken down into three domains, the first of which has several subdomains.

Domain I: Provision of individualized nutrition support care to patients

- **Subdomain A:** Assessment (17% of exam)
- **Subdomain B:** Development and implementation of a therapeutic plan (22% of exam)
- **Subdomain C:** Monitoring and management (39% of exam)

Domain II: Management of nutrition support services (13% of exam)

Domain III: Advancement of nutrition support pharmacy practice (9% of exam)

The following is a sample question from the examination:

A well-nourished 36-year-old male was transferred to the surgical ICU [intensive care unit] following an exploratory laparotomy for a gunshot wound to the abdomen. Transfer orders included continuous nasogastric suction, IM morphine for pain, cefoxitin 2gm IVPB q8 hrs. and D5-Normal Saline, 85ml/hr. On admission to the SICU, his serum electrolytes were normal. The patient remained NPO because of continued intestinal ileus, the nasogastric suction volume averaged 2000 ml daily, and the patient's weight was unchanged. Laboratory values on the third post-op day were:

Sodium 137 mEQ/L   (normal 135–147)
Potassium 3.8 mEq/L   (normal 3.5–5.0)
Chloride 89 mEqL   (normal 95–105)

CO3 37 mEq/L   (normal 22–28)
Glucose 111 mg/dL   (normal 70–110)
BUN 22 mg/dL   (normal 8–18)
Creatinine 1.2 mg/dL (normal 0.6–1.2)

Which of the following therapeutic recommendations is appropriate at this time?
1. Initiate TPN due to prolonged period on NPO status
2. Initiate parenteral ranitidine therapy to reduce gastric acidity
3. Increase IV infusion rate to match nasogastric output volume
4. Change IV infusion to D5-Lactated Ringers at same infusion rate

Correct answer: 2

BPS certified pharmacist specialists are recognized for their advanced level of knowledge, skills, and achievement by many government agencies and educational organizations. Increasing numbers of employers are recognizing BPS-certified specialists with monetary rewards or promotion/hiring preferences.

INTERVIEW WITH DR. JACQUELINE BARBER

Jacqueline Barber earned a bachelor of science degree in human nutrition in 1979, and a bachelor of science degree in pharmacy in 1981, both from the University of Minnesota. In 1983, she earned her doctor of pharmacy degree from the University of Texas Health Sciences Center in San Antonio. Returning to the University of Minnesota, she completed training as an AHSP (Academy of Health-Systems Professionals) Fellow in pharmacy nutrition support in 1984. She is presently a pharmacy clinical specialist in nutrition support at Methodist Hospital in Minneapolis and a preceptor for Pharm.D. students from the University of Minnesota. She teaches courses in clinical nutrition at the college and via the Internet through Outreach Education. She has been board certified in pharmacy nutrition support since 1993. Highlights from an interview with Dr. Barber follow.

Question: *What is a BCNSP?*
Dr. Barber: *A board certified nutrition support pharmacist is one who has taken and passed an examination in the specialty of nutrition support. In order to qualify for the examination, the individual must be able to demonstrate experience and/or evidence of training in pharmacy nutrition support. The exam is not easy, either!*

Question: *Could you give a brief summary of educational pathways to gain BCNSP status?*
Dr. Barber: *The first step is a pharmacy degree, either a BS for the people who have been in practice for a while, or more typically, a [Pharm.D.] degree. The doctor of pharmacy is now offered in most, if not all, schools of pharmacy. Many people then receive extra training during a residency and/or fellowship, in which they may do at least a portion of their work in specialized nutrition support (enteral and parenteral nutrition). These experiences can last one to three years. If they do not take up this kind of training, then several years of work experience in this area may also be used in the application for the examination.*

Question: *Is there such a thing as a "typical day" on the job?*
Dr. Barber: *No. BCNSPs may work in any setting in which you find pharmacists and patients who need nutrition support. This includes hospitals, home care settings, industry, sometimes clinic settings, and, of course, schools of pharmacy. For those of us in clinical practice, the typical day may involve a review of a patient's*

orders or laboratory and clinical status; discussion with the patient or dietary, nursing, or medical staff; adjustments of orders or monitoring parameters (labs); and working in the pharmacy to prepare the nutrition regimen for the patient.

Question: *What is the outlook for employment in the future for students interested in being BCNSPs?*

Dr. Barber: *Since pharmacists have been in short supply the last few years, many BCNSPs are involved in activities in addition to nutrition support. There are a number of people in well-known programs, usually affiliated with a university and teaching programs, who are truly specialists and may also be involved in research. Others are in home care and may manage other forms of IV therapy in addition to nutrition support. Then there are those who have clinical activities and some teaching activities. There are many variations. It is safe to say at this point that there are positions out there for pharmacists to be involved in nutritional activities, but many pharmacists are involved in various types of pharmacy activities and may do nutrition as part of this mix.*

Question: *Where will most of the jobs be in the future?*

Dr. Barber: *Home care continues to be a growing area.*

SALARY AND BENEFITS

RDs who specialize in nutrition support have training beyond the basic clinical dietitian training and have usually had several years of work experience. They are therefore paid at the upper end of the pay scale for RDs—$50,000 or more per year. If they work for a company that produces TPN or enteral nutrition solutions, they may receive higher salaries.

Most pharmacists working in this area have Pharm.D. degrees with additional training. In 2001, the median salary for a pharmacist in the United States was about $74,000 with a range of salaries from $53,900 to $85,200 per year. Again, pharmacists working for companies who manufacture TPN may receive higher salaries.

Unless self-employed, most nutrition support professionals get a full range of benefits, including paid vacations and holidays, retirement packages, and health insurance.

WORK ENVIRONMENT

Most nutrition support personnel work in hospitals or out-patient facilities, which have pleasant surroundings and state-of-the-art equipment. Those who work in critical care units may find the work environment to be stressful. Patients needing parenteral or enteral nutrition have chronic problems that the nutritionist must address, so a significant amount of time may be spent in listening and teaching. Weekend, night, and holiday work may be necessary as problems can arise at any time. This "call" work is usually shared by team members. With the advent of home TPN/TF, nutrition support dietitians may make house calls seeing that a patient's parenteral or enteral nutrition delivery system equipment is functioning properly and troubleshooting to avoid unexpected problems. This may require a considerable amount of travel.

CHAPTER 6

CHEF

O n first glance, the inclusion of a chapter on chefs in a book on nutrition careers may seem out of place. However, chefs are, and have always been, interested in the nutritional aspects of food as well as its preparation and presentation. Fully aware of the increasing incidence of obesity in this country, many chefs are preparing exciting meals while paying close attention to calorie and fat content. Menus are increasingly presenting "heart-smart" choices.

Joseph M. Carlin, in the March 1998 issue of *Nutrition Today*, tells of Mrs. N. K. M. Lee, a professed Boston housekeeper. In 1832, Mrs. Lee wrote *The Cook's Own Book*, a collection of more than 2,000 recipes. Lee wrote that "the cook should be much elevated in public estimation" and that cooks should "form a strict alliance with the physician." She went on to say, "The cook exercises a greater power over the public health and welfare than the physician."

The complexity of a chef's job depends on where he or she is located in the hierarchy of the culinary arts. At the top of the ladder are the certified master chefs (CMC). With the recent addition of three new certified master chefs, the American Culinary Federation reports that there are now seventy certified master chefs in the United States. Master chefs direct the work of executive chefs and other lesser chefs in very prestigious restaurants and in major corporations. They are frequently teachers in top-ranked culinary schools and consultants to various food companies. They may be restaurant or resort owners.

Certified executive chefs (CECs) are in charge of large kitchens or perhaps multiple kitchens if they are employed by restaurant chains. They oversee the operation of the entire establishment and have ultimate responsibility for everything that happens there. They may do many of the same things done by a food service manager, including menu planning, development and maintenance of standards for the preparation and serving of food; purchasing, costing, and inventory of food; and training and supervision of other food service workers. In addition to all of that, they cook.

Chefs de cuisine are the "head cooks" in the kitchen. The actual responsibility of cooking food falls to them and to others whom they supervise. They may carry out other duties assigned to them by the executive chef, but their chief responsibility is cooking. Sous chefs (underchefs) work under the chef de cuisine. Sous chefs may share responsibilities for training those who work under them and for other administrative duties at the request of their supervisors. Chefs de parties are line cooks who are responsible for preparing specific menu items. They may specialize in particular types of food preparation and have names particular to that specialty—saucier, for instance.

A chef's job also varies with the type of establishment in which he or she works. Those working for large institutions like hospitals, schools, or prisons have special challenges of cooking nutritious food in large quantities.

Many of these organizations now employ institutional food services rather than maintain their own kitchens and food service workers.

Chefs in restaurants have different challenges. While the quantity of food they prepare may not be as great, they must have the capability of producing a variety of dishes that can be served to many patrons at the same time. The reputation of the restaurant sits directly on the shoulders of the chefs and how successful they are in meeting those challenges.

FORECAST FOR THE FUTURE

The BLS says that more than 2.8 million people worked in food service jobs in 2000. Of these, 5,200 were chefs working in private households, and 139,000 were chefs or head cooks in restaurants or other facilities. Job openings for chefs and other food service workers will be plentiful through 2010 with employment growth being spurred by increases in population, household income, and leisure time. The convenience and pleasure of dining out is an offshoot of these changes.

Employment in fast-food chains is expected to decrease while jobs for trained chefs in full-service restaurants will increase. This is prompted to some extent by the aging of the population. Those over age fifty-five have more money to spend in restaurants and prefer to go to places with good service, a nice ambience, and great food.

EDUCATION, TRAINING, AND OTHER CERTIFICATION

There are more than 3,000 cooking schools in the United States. In an article entitled "Learning to Serve, Serving to Learn: An Introduction to Cooking Schools and Culinary Institutes," W. Randy Hoffman identifies four categories of schools for those interested in becoming chefs. The first are schools dedicated strictly to cooking and culinary institutes. Perhaps the best known school of this type in the United States is the Culinary Institute of America (CIA). A degree from the CIA is considered the gold standard against which other degrees in the culinary arts are compared. CIA offers both an associate's degree in occupational studies (AOS) and a bachelor's of professional studies in culinary arts (BPS), as well as other nondegree programs.

The goals of the twenty-one-month-long program leading to the AOS degree are listed on the Web site of CIA (http://www.ciachef.edu). They include:

- Development of proficiency in classic and contemporary culinary techniques and cooking methods in a la carte, table d'hote, and banquet settings.
- Preparation of American, Asian, and other international cuisines.
- Learning basic baking, and exploration of nutrition, menu development, food safety, writing, communication, and cost control.
- Gaining practical experience in an eighteen-week paid externship.

A sample curriculum for this program is also listed on the Web site (see Table 6-1 on the following page). The school year is broken into blocks of time with specific subjects being taken in each block. All blocks in the freshman and sophomore years are three weeks long except for block B (six weeks) and block K (eighteen weeks).

The bachelor of professional studies in culinary arts builds on the courses and experience of the AOS curriculum. (Refer to Table 6-2 on page 75 for a sample curriculum.) In addition to the goals set for the AOS degree, other goals of this program are:

- To explore diverse languages, history, and culinary traditions

Table 6-1: Sample Curriculum

Culinary Institute of America
Associate Degree in Occupational Studies-Culinary Art

Block Subjects Studied

Freshman Year, First Semester

A	Mathematics Fundamentals (noncredit), Writing Fundamentals (noncredit)
B	Introduction to Gastronomy, Mathematics, Product Knowledge, Food Safety, Introduction to Computers (non-credit, elective)
C	Meat Identification and Fabrication, Seafood Identification and Fabrication
D	Skill Development I
E	Skill Development II

Writing is taught throughout all blocks this semester.

Freshman Year, Second Semester

F	Skill Development III
G	Cuisines of the Americas, Writing Examination
H	Cuisines of Asia, Costing Examination
I	Lunch Cookery, Breakfast Cookery
J	Garde Manger (preparing cold meat dishes and garnishing), cooking examination

Introduction to interpersonal communication is taught throughout all blocks this semester.

K	Externship During Summer

Sophomore Year, First Semester

L	Nutrition, Introduction to Management, Menu Development, Controlling Costs and Purchasing Food, Restaurant Law (noncredit)
M	Baking and Pastry Skill Development
N	Cuisines of Europe and the Mediterranean
O	Wines and Beverages

Sophomore Year, Second Semester

P	Banqueting and Catering, Costing Examination
Q	Italian Cuisine, Nutritional Cooking
R	Introductory Table Service, Cooking Examination
S	Advanced Restaurant Cooking
T	Advanced Table Service

- To discover how to make a culinary business profitable by studying marketing, computers, and finance.

- To learn how to best work with and supervise others through such courses as interpersonal communications, psychology, ethics, and management.

The second category of school listed by W. Randy Hoffman is the career school. These schools offer vocational training that prepares students for a variety of occupations. Examples are Johnson and Wales University (J & W) and the Career Education Corporation (CEC), both of which have multiple campuses across the country where students can study culinary sciences as well as other topics. J & W offers both an associate in science (AS) degree and a bachelor of science (BS) degree in the culinary arts. They say that their AS degree "provides students with practical education in food production while developing professionalism and excellence in academic achievement. Students progress through a program of study that builds proficiency in food production and cooking, cost control, nutrition, sanitation, and food marketing. Hands-on training is paired with traditional academic courses resulting in a curriculum that is both dynamic and directly aligned with industry needs."

The first-year curriculum for this program includes mathematics, introduction to life science, English composition, community service, professional development, sanitation, basic cooking and baking methods, beverage and dining room service, and national certification in alcohol intervention procedures. Courses for the second year of the program include foundations of leadership, personalized nutrition management, communication skills, introduction to menu planning and cost control, as well as advanced techniques in classical/international cuisines, garde manger, patisserie/dessert, and dining room. The second year is followed by a culinary arts internship at university-owned hotels and restaurants, including the Radisson Airport Hotel and the Johnson and

Table 6-2: Sample Curriculum
Culinary Institute of America
Bachelor of Professional Studies in Culinary Arts

The first two years of the BPS program are spent in the same courses offered in the AOS program.

Junior Year, First Semester	Junior Year, Second Semester
Composition and Communications	Accounting and Budget Management
Computers in the Food Business	Computers in the Food Business II
Economics	French, Italian, or Spanish II
French, Italian, or Spanish I	History and Culture of Europe
Interpersonal Communications	Marketing and Promoting Foods
	Psychology of Human Behavior
Intersession (six weeks)	
	Wine and Food Seminar

Senior Year, First Semester	Senior Year, Second Semester
Advanced Cooking	Restaurant Operations
Financial Management	Ethics
French, Italian, or Spanish III	French, Italian, or Spanish IV
History and Culture of the Americas	History and Culture of Asia
Human Resource Management	Managing Quality for the Future
	Food and Culture or
	Professional Food Writing
	or World Literature,
	or Business Planning,
	or Field Experience and Action Plan,
	or Senior Thesis, Culinary Arts
	Wine and Food Seminar

Wales Inn, where students participate in actual public food service operations.

J & W's bachelor of science degree program prepares candidates for careers as executive chefs. The program combines practical education in food production with leadership training and general studies courses. It provides students with the opportunity to increase cognitive, critical thinking, and practical application skills. Students will attend three terms of academic studies. In both the junior and senior years, students will attend intensive advanced laboratories designed to build leadership, planning, and evaluation skills. They will also have hands-on experience in proper cooking and baking techniques, ice carving, creative garnishing, plate presentation, and the cuisines of the world.

Other opportunities offered in this program are a one-term advanced career cooperative education program, which places students with chefs in famous restaurants and resorts. This term may be replaced with a summer term abroad studying regional wines and cuisines.

Hoffman's third category of culinary schools are traditional colleges and universities. Community colleges, vocational schools, and junior colleges may provide two-year programs leading to certification in the culinary arts. Four-year courses in colleges and universities offer baccalaureate degrees with an emphasis in the culinary arts, hospitality, or other similar degrees. Kendall College in Evanston, Illinois, is an example of a small liberal arts college that has a strong program in the culinary arts. Its School of Culinary Arts at Kendall College is a nationally acclaimed culinary program. It offers associate's and bachelor's degree programs as well as certificates in Baking and Pastry, Professional Catering, Professional Personal Chef, and Professional Cookery.

The associate of applied science in culinary arts (AAS) degree requires the successful completion of ninety-six credit hours. The bachelor of arts (BA) degree expands on the AAS degree. The first two years of the two programs are the same. Refer to Table 6-3 on pages 78 and 79 for a sample curriculum.

Hoffman's last category is the recreational cooking school. These can be found on cruise ships, in department stores, at local churches, or in any number of other places that offer relative short courses in cooking.

One such school is the Natural Gourmet Institute for Food and Health in New York City, which was founded in 1977 by Anne Marie Corban, a firm believer in health-supportive cooking. She established a chef's training program in 1985, and now trains 144 students per year in the preparation and cooking of natural foods. The course offered at the school requires 600 hours of cooking instruction and practical experience. Most graduates of the course are employed in natural food establishments or become private chefs or caterers specializing in health-conscious cooking. The institute also offers a variety of classes in vegetarian cooking techniques, gluten-free baking, and cooking with herbs. Applicants for this school must have a high school diploma or GED.

A category of culinary education not mentioned by Hoffman is that offered by various branches of the military. For instance, many chefs begin their cooking careers at the Army Center of Excellence in Fort Lee, Virginia, with the Basic Food Service Specialist Course (BFSSC). Heike Hasenauer reports in an online article entitled "Cultivating Chefs" that 5,000 new cooks are trained each year through this program. Seventy-five percent are enlisted army personnel and 25 percent are marines. After eight weeks of intensive training, new cooks are assigned to dining facilities throughout the world.

Initially, students prepare one to five servings of various dishes. In the second phase of training, they must prepare portions for 50 to 100 or more people.

INTERVIEW WITH DENNIS ADAMS

SFC Dennis Adams, a retired army mess sergeant, received his culinary training in the army. The following are highlights from an interview with Sgt. Adams.

Question: *Why did you decide to apply for cooking school when you entered the army?*

Sgt. Adams: *As all enlisted men know, you draw a lot of KP [kitchen patrol] when you're a private. Although KP involved a lot of peeling and not much cooking, I found*

Table 6-3: Sample Curriculum

The School of Culinary Arts at Kendall College
AAS & BA in Culinary Arts

First Term (Quarter)	Credits
Introduction to Professional Cookery	2
Introduction to Soups, Stocks, and Sauces	2
Introduction to Garde Manger	2
Introduction to Methods of Cooking	2
Sanitation	0
Composition	4
Math	4

Second Term (Quarter)	
Resume/Interviewing and Internship Prep	1
Quantity Food Production	3
Product ID	2
Storeroom	2
Computers in the Restaurant Industry	2
Cost Control	2
Advanced Skills	2
Human Nutrition	4

Third Term (Quarter)	
Introduction to Bread Baking	3
Introduction to Pastry	3
Introduction to Dining Room Service	3
Spanish	4
Ethics	4

Fourth Term (Quarter)	
Internship	12
Composition II	4

Fifth Term (Quarter)	
Food Service Management	4
Advanced Garde Manger	3
Advanced Sauce and Fish	3
Social Science Elective	4

Sixth Term (Quarter) — Credits

	Credits
Catering or Symposium	2
French Classical, Regional Cuisine	3
American Cuisine	3
Facility Planning	4

Those advancing on for the BA degree take the following
courses during the next two years:

Junior Year, Term 1

Cuisine of Asia	4
Math	4
Political and Legal Issues of Food Service	4
Advanced Pastry I	2

Junior Year, Term 2

Cuisine of Central America	4
Spanish II	4
Marketing Principles	4
Food History	4

Junior Year, Term 3

Cuisine of the Mediterranean	4
Spanish III	4
Principles of Economics	4
Social Science Requirement	4

Senior Year, Term 1

Food Science	4
Basic Speech	4
Organizational Behavior	4
Math	4

Senior Year, Term 2

Research and Development	4
Techniques of Persuasion	4
Wines, Spirits, and Affinities	4
Culinary Managerial Accounting	4

Senior Year, Term 3

Labor Relations	4
Food Service PR and the Chef	4
Special Events Operations and Sales	4
Advanced Pastry II	2
Capstone Project	0

that I really was interested in cooking. When I reenlisted after my first two years of active duty, I was sent to cooking school. At that time, military cooks, regardless of branch of service, were trained in whatever cooking school was opened at the time they were assigned. I happened to be sent to McConnell Air Force Base in Wichita, Kansas, for my training. Now, all army cooks, who are members of the Quartermaster Corps, are trained at Ft. Lee, Virginia, which is the Quartermaster Corps Headquarters.

Question: *How long was your training course and what did it involve?*

Sgt. Adams: *Cooking school lasted for nine weeks. The first week involved book work, learning to use stoves, ovens, and various kinds of field equipment. We didn't actually start cooking until the second week of the course. We started out with pretty simple and basic dishes and progressed to more complicated things. At the end of the course, we were given a large file drawer containing hundreds of recipes. The minimum number each one of these recipes serves is 100, so if I want to use one of these recipes today, I have to cut the recipe a lot.*

Question: *What was your first assignment after finishing school?*

Sgt. Adams: *I was assigned to work in a basic training unit at Ft. Leonard Wood, Missouri. I think this was because the soldiers in basic training units would not consider complaining about the food. In that job, I cooked for thirty days in the field every sixty days. When cooking in the field, only breakfast and dinner are hot meals. The noon meal is "C-rations" or what are now called Meals Ready to Eat (MRE). We served about 250 to 300 soldiers at each meal. I was then sent to Germany where I cooked for three years. After again reenlisting, I spent another two years in Germany. By* *this time, I was first cook and was responsible for cooking most of the meats and supervising other cooks in the preparation of the rest of the meal. I finished my tour of duty with two years in Okinawa [in Japan]. Most of the cooks there were Japanese. I was the supervisor.*

Question: *Is the hierarchy for cooks in the military the same as for chefs in civilian life?*
Sgt. Adams: *Well, there is definitely a hierarchy. The lowest level is cook's helper followed in ascending order by cook, first cook, mess sergeant, then dining facility manager. I guess a dining facility manager would be similar to an executive chef.*

Question: *Did you continue your career in the military?*
Sgt. Adams: *After a short break from the regular military, I joined the reserves and when I retired after twenty-six years was a sergeant first class and mess sergeant for my unit.*

Question: *What changes did you notice in your years as a military cook?*
Sgt. Adams: *In the [1960s] when I started cooking, the army's philosophy was "Soldiers travel on their stomach, feed them a lot." The people planning the menus were mostly men who were meat and potato folks, so we served a lot of starch and grilled or fried meats. By the [1970s], dietitians, mostly women, were making a real impact on military menus. The meat and potato philosophy fell by the wayside and was replaced with well-rounded menus with many foods being steamed or broiled rather than fried. My goal as a military cook was to always serve the best meals. I have won several awards through the years for the quality of my cooking.*

Question: *Have you done any professional cooking since leaving the military?*

Sgt. Adams: *Yes, I owned my own restaurant and bar for a while and also worked as a cook in the Ponca City, Oklahoma, school system for a year. Now, I cook for my family and friends and still enjoy being in the kitchen.*

Question: *Do you have any advice for students who are considering the culinary arts and/or military careers?*

Sgt. Adams: *I think the military is a good place to grow up. If you are thinking about going to college but are unsure what you really want to do, the military gives you a place to find yourself. If you are interested in cooking, being a military cook is a great option. Believe it or not, the pay of an army cook is better than the salary of most civilian cooks or chefs. If you stick with it, you also qualify for great retirement pay and benefits.*

THE AMERICAN CULINARY FEDERATION

The American Culinary Federation (ACF) is a professional organization. It was founded in 1929 to promote the professional image of American chefs worldwide through education among culinarians at all levels. The ACF helps set professional standards for culinary education and assists in career development. It operates the only comprehensive certification program for chefs in the United States. It sponsors more than eighty culinary and pastry apprenticeship programs around the country. Programs are three years long and are held in family-owned restaurants, resort hotels, and many prestigious hotel restaurants.

The requirements of the apprenticeships include 192 hours of classroom work each year for three years. These technical courses are usually taken at a community college working in partnership with a chapter of the American Culinary Federation.

The second requirement of the apprenticeships is a total of 6,000 hours of on-the-job training in the three-year period. These hours may be spent in the kitchens of restaurants, resorts, or institutions that are working in conjunction with the local ACF chapter.

The ACF also accredits programs in secondary and vocational culinary arts programs. Graduates of these programs must take an ACF culinary proficiency test to receive certification. Many of these graduates go on to apprenticeship programs or ACF-certified college culinary programs.

Certification programs are also offered by the Research Chefs Association (RCA). RCA was founded in 1996 to develop a certification program for chefs working in the food industry. The University of Nebraska and Metropolitan Community College in Omaha, Nebraska, working with the RCA, have developed both two- and four-year degree programs in culinology. Culinology, a term trademarked by the RCA, is defined as "a blending of culinary arts and food science." Jeff Cousminor, director of savory product and flavor development for Firmenich, Inc., in an October 2003 teleforum for members of the Food and Culinary Professionals dietetic practice group of the ADA, says that courses in these culinology programs are equally divided among general education classes, culinary courses, and food science and nutrition courses. He believes there will be at least ten such courses offered across the country within three to five years. Two certification programs are now offered by the RCA. One is certified research chef for chefs with food service backgrounds, and the other is certified culinary scientists for those with a culinary background.

Regardless of the route taken in becoming a chef, the single most important ingredient in having a successful career as a chef is a love of cooking. Alejandro Granes, a former line cook at the Omni William Penn Hotel in Pittsburgh, Pennsylvania, told W. Randy Hoffman, "You have to love the kitchen, to love preparing the food. You can have all the skills in the world, but if your heart's not in it, it's no good."

SALARY AND BENEFITS

The BLS says that the wages of chefs depend greatly on the part of the country and type of establishment in which chefs are employed. Wages are highest in elegant restaurants and hotels where many executive chefs are employed. Median hourly earnings of head cooks and chefs were $12.07 per hour in 2000. The range of salaries was $7.39 per hour to $22.77 per hour. Salaries for master chefs and executive chefs are much higher.

Wages for lesser chefs and cooks in chain restaurants, fast-food restaurants, long-term care facilities, prisons, schools, hospitals, and other institutions ranged from $7.52 per hour to $9.97 per hour in 2000.

Other benefits vary widely with the institution for which a chef works. Some provide uniforms or uniform allowances. Most executive chefs and lesser chefs working in hotels or resort kitchens full-time receive a full range of benefits, including paid holidays and vacations, health insurance, and retirement plans.

WORK ENVIRONMENT

Master and executive chefs frequently work in pleasant offices equipped with state-of-the-art computer equipment when not in the kitchen. Many restaurant and institutional kitchens have modern equipment and convenient work areas, and are well air-conditioned. Many kitchens, however, may be older, smaller, and poorly equipped. The job requires spending many hours on your feet, a considerable amount of heavy lifting, and night, weekend, and holiday work. There is some risk of burns, cuts, and other injuries for those who work in kitchens.

CHAPTER 7

DIETETIC TECHNICIAN, REGISTERED

Using a military analogy, a dietetic technician, registered (DTR) can be compared to a master sergeant—the person who really gets things done. According to the ADA, DTRs are an integral part of the health-care and food-service management team. They typically work under the direction of a registered dietitian but, like the master sergeant, use skills and training to independently accomplish the goals of the team.

Working closely with an RD, a dietetic technician helps to assess, plan, implement, and evaluate nutrition plans for patients in hospitals, long-term care facilities, and other institutions. In addition, the DTR may assume varying degrees of responsibility for food-service operations. This may include menu planning, recipe development, and supervision of the people working in the food service. It is common for a DTR to become the interface between food-service personnel and the dietitian who is directing the service. In this capacity, the DTR may be responsible for the development of work schedules, keeping track of the hours worked by those in the food service, and be the first responder if personnel problems arise. This requires the DTR to have exceptional people skills to keep things running smoothly.

A DTR is also an educator, responsible for helping people understand their own nutritional needs and how diet plans meet those needs. Under the direction of the dietitian, DTRs work with patients with diabetes, heart disease, and other medical conditions that require patients to pay close attention to their diets to maximize the quality of their lives. They may also assist or be responsible for training of food service personnel and may act as mentors and supervisors for students training in nutrition and dietetic sciences.

Dietetic technicians may also be employed by food companies to help develop new foods that are tasty as well as nutritious. People who are talented salespeople and have strong backgrounds in nutrition are especially attractive in the food industry. Opportunities may also be available in colleges and universities at both the food service level and in research projects.

FORECAST FOR THE FUTURE

As with other careers in nutrition and dietetics, employment opportunities are expected to increase at least through 2010. In 2000, there were approximately 25,600 DTRs in the United States. By 2010, there are expected to be almost 33,000. The average number of job openings in the field each year is 1,370.

Traditionally, most dietetic technicians have been employed in hospitals. However, with the trend away from inpatient hospital care, technicians will find better employment opportunities in long-term care facilities, schools, correctional institutions, and in industry. Institutional food service companies that contract with hospitals and other institutions to provide food services also have positions available for DTRs.

INTERVIEW WITH DENISE ELMORE

Denise Elmore was recently named Texas Dietetic Technician of the Year. She is the chair of the ADA's Dietetic Practice Group #45, Dietetic Technicians in Practice (DTP). Elmore's interest in nutrition began at age fifteen when she worked as a dietary aide in a nursing home. She eventually earned an associate's degree in nutrition and went on to become a dietetic technician, registered. In an interview, Ms. Elmore gave insights helpful to students considering careers as dietetic technicians.

Question: *Would you please describe your present job?*

Ms. Elmore: *I am currently a junior research coordinator in the Nutrition Group for the Department of Epidemiology in the Division of Cancer Prevention at the University of Texas M.D. Anderson Cancer Center. Basically the job I do now is coordinating the research data that is compiled for twelve cancer studies we are providing support for in our department. I assist with writing grants, developing nutrition questionnaires, and writing computer codes to set up data-entry screens. I train (data-entry) operators, interview staff, process data, run analyses, write papers and abstracts, and present posters, etc. Four years ago, my nutrition group at UTMDACC wanted to add a position and that is how the job was created for me. They didn't have funding for an RD, so naturally a DTR was the perfect choice.*

Question: *Have you had training beyond your associate's degree that has helped you with this job?*

Ms. Elmore: *I do have a bachelor's degree in business administration. I am the only DTR here or in the United States currently doing this level of research. I have won* *numerous awards here in Houston, Texas, and at ADA. I was featured, along with three other DTRs, in the November [2003] issue of the* Journal of the American Dietetics Association *for my innovative job.*

Question: *What do you like most about your job?*

Ms. Elmore: *The best thing about my job is that in my area of practice, growth and knowledge are encouraged. I think many DTRs don't get adequate encouragement to learn more, so they become stunted and in dead-end jobs with no advancement. My job also encourages me to think outside the normal box or outside the parameters of what a DTR usually does. The RDs with whom I work are constantly encouraging me and assisting me with any expressed desire for knowledge. But then again, I am in an academic arena.*

Question: *In general, how has the trend toward shorter inpatient hospital stays affected DTRs?*

Ms. Elmore: *I do know that the trends for shorter stays in the hospital are not affecting DTR jobs as much as they are affecting the RDs. In most hospitals here in Texas, the DTRs are the ones who do most of the nutrition screening processes. I have seen several hospitals downsize the number of RDs and increase the number of DTRs. We are historically cheaper to hire and have the right amount of nutrition background for the nutritional screening processes. Then the RDs focus on only the high acuity patients.*

EDUCATION, TRAINING, AND OTHER QUALIFICATIONS

Most programs for DTRs recommend that high school students interested in the field obtain a well-rounded education while in high school. They should take at least two courses in mathematics. At least one biology and one chemistry course are mandatory. Writing and good communication skills are important to a DTR, so English courses that emphasize writing are helpful. As with almost any profession today, computer skills are very important. Most programs require that a candidate have a high school diploma or GED.

The Commission on Dietetic Registration lists two pathways by which persons may become eligible for certification as a dietetic technician. The first pathway requires completion of an associate degree granted by a college or university that provides a CADE-accredited Dietetics Technician Program. These programs include 450 hours of supervised practical experience in various community programs in health care, and food-service facilities. There are seventy such CADE-approved programs in the United States. Baltimore City Community College's Dietetic Technician Program in Maryland is one of the seventy programs. Refer to Table 7-1 on page 90 for a sample curriculum.

Penn State University offers a nontraditional option for obtaining training to complete the requirements to become a DTR. It offers a dietetic food systems management associate's degree through a distance education program. Students enrolled in this and similar programs are not burdened with the expense of attending college full time. They can work at their own speed from their homes and can continue to hold paying jobs while they complete the program. They have ready access to one-on-one counseling by registered dietitians from the school's faculty.

Penn State's program consists of twenty-two courses, which the student works on with the aid of textbooks, a study guide with lesson assignments, and other materials. Some of the courses require workplace experience, which is supervised by an approved proctor or mentor. To be eligible for this program, a student must be employed at least fifteen hours per week in a health-care food-service facility. The student is also responsible for finding a registered dietitian to serve as a mentor.

Table 7-1: Sample Curriculum

Baltimore City Community College
Dietetic Technician Program (Associate Degree)

Course	Credits
First Semester	
AH116 Food Service Sanitation Management	1
DNT 110 Orientation to Dietetics	1
DNT 113 Food Service Management I	3
DNT 114 Foods	4
Total	8
Second Semester	
DNT 121 Dietetic Field Experience I	2
DNT 123 Food Service Management II	3
DNT 124 Normal Nutrition	3
Total	8
Third Semester	
AH 130 Medical Terminology	3
DNT 232 Dietetic Field Experience II	2
DNT 233 Food Service Management III	3
Total	8
Fourth Semester	
BIO 111 Anatomy and Physiology I	4
DNT 234 Applied Nutrition	3
DNT 242 Dietetic Field Experience III	2
Total	9
Fifth Semester	
BIO 112 Anatomy and Physiology II	4
DNT 244 Medical Nutrition Therapy	3
DNT 252 Dietetic Field Experience IV	2
Total	9
Sixth Semester	
DNT 240 Dietetic Seminar	1
DNT 243 Food Service Management IV	3
DNT 262 Dietetic Field Experience V	2
HIT 251 Health Care Management and Supervision	3
Total	9

In addition to these classes, students must complete the following courses prior to the fifth semester:

ENG 101 English Writing	3
MATH General Education Requirements: Math	2
PE Physical Education	3
PSY 101 Introduction to Psychology	3
SOC 101 Introduction to Sociology	3
SP 101 Introduction to Speech	3–4
Total	17–18

The second pathway was developed for people who have completed baccalaureate degrees from an accredited college or university but who wish to become dietetic technicians. These people must complete a CADE Didactic Program in Dietetics and a CADE-accredited dietetic technician supervised practice.

Successful completion of courses of study in either of these pathways qualifies a candidate for the dietetic technician registration examination, which DTR candidates must successfully complete. The Registration Examination for Dietetic Technicians evaluates the dietetic technician's ability to perform at an entry level. The examination content domains and topics listed in Table 7-2 on page 92 are based on the 2000 CDR Dietetics Practice Audit.

The following are sample examination questions from the *Registration Examination for Dietetic Technicians Handbook for Candidates*.

1. A recent *E. coli* outbreak could have been avoided if the tainted hamburger had been
    A. Frozen at 0 degrees F for 2 days.
    B. Cooked to 155 degrees F.
    C. Cooked at 145 degrees F.
    D. Defrosted in a microwave oven.

2. A dietetic technician is asked to present a program at a congregate meal site. The audience is elderly and may have cardiovascular disease. The importance of a low-fat, low-cholesterol diet must be emphasized. The most effective method of presentation includes a
    A. Game to identify high-cholesterol, high-fat foods.
    B. Movies that show the effects of high-fat diets on arteries.
    C. Slide programs on the preparation of meals low in fat and cholesterol.
    D. Lectures that emphasize the health hazards of fat and cholesterol.

Table 7-2		

Registration Examination for Dietetics Technicians
Test Specifications, Effective September 1, 2002

Content of Examination	Percent of Exam
I. Food and Nutrition	10%
A. Principles of Food Preparation and Food Supply	
B. Nutrient Composition of Food	
C. Principles of Normal Diet	
II. Nutrition Services: Community/Clinical	38%
A. Basic Nutrition Screening and Assessment	
B. Applied Normal Nutrition/Health Promotion/Disease Prevention	
C. Medical Nutrition Therapy	
III. Counseling, Education, and Training	7%
A. Assessment and Planning	
B. Implementation and Evaluation	
IV. Food Service Systems	25%
A. Menu Planning	
B. Procurement and Materials Management	
C. Food Production, Distribution, Service, and Facility Design	
D. Safety and Sanitation	
V. Management	20%
A. Human Resources	
B. Finance and Materials	
C. Marketing Products and Services	
D. Principles and Processes	
E. Quality Improvement and Research	

3. The average daily intake of an eighteen-year-old man is 95 g of protein, 98 g of fat, and 260 g of carbohydrate. What is the average daily intake of Kcal?
   A. 1,873
   B. 2,010
   C. 2,302
   D. 2,704

Answer key: 1. B; 2. A; 3. C.

Like the registration exam for RDs, this computer-based exam is given at many different testing sites throughout the United States Monday through Friday of each week and on Saturdays at some sites. It is scored immediately and candidates are given their scores on the day of the exam. Successful candidates receive registration certificates and are entitled to use the initials "DTR" after their names. To maintain registration, DTRs must take continuing professional education courses.

SALARY AND BENEFITS

According to the ADA's 2002 Membership Benefit Survey, the median hourly wage for a DTR was $14.74 per hour or about $30,600 per year. Variability in salaries reflects years of experience, responsibilities, employment setting, and the scope of the practice. BLS data shows that in 2001, the median annual salary for a DTR was $21,800 with a range of $14,000 to $34,700 per year.

Benefit packages also reflect job variability. Most DTRs receive paid holidays and vacations, health insurance, and pension plan options. Many also have free meals available during working hours.

WORK ENVIRONMENT

Most DTRs work in clean, well-lit, modern facilities with up-to-date equipment. The job is a very active one and requires a lot of walking and standing. Weekend and holiday work may be necessary, but most DTRs work a regular forty-hour week.

CHAPTER 8

FOOD SCIENTIST

The Institute of Food Technologists defines food science as "the discipline in which the engineering, biological, and physical sciences are used to study the nature of foods, the causes of deterioration, the principles underlying food processing, and the improvement of food for the consuming public." It defines food technology as "the application of food science to the selection, preservation, processing, packaging, distribution and use of safe, nutritious, and wholesome foods." Therefore, food scientists or technologists are people who apply scientific and engineering principles in research and development, production, packaging, and the processing of foods.

Food scientists working in research and development study the chemical changes that take place in stored or processed foods. They try to find ways to process and store foods so that fewer nutrients are lost. They also study the effects of food additives on the nutritional quality and safety of foods. Above all, food scientists are constantly seeking new ways to keep food safe from microorganisms that can contaminate food, making it deadly if eaten.

INTERVIEW WITH VICKIE KLOERIS

Actual job responsibilities vary considerably with the position that the food scientist holds. Take, for instance, food scientist Vickie Kloeris, who works for the National Aeronautics and Space Administration (NASA). Her official title is shuttle and ISS (International Space Station) food systems manager. In an article on NASA Quest, NASA's educational Web site, which profiles some of the men and women who work for NASA, Ms. Kloeris answers questions about her job and the training she has had in food science.

Question: *What is your present job?*

Ms. Kloeris: *I am responsible for all the food that is sent into orbit to the shuttle and the space station. We have two different contractors who provide food—one for the shuttle and one for the space station. I am the NASA interface [liaison] to each of these contractors, and it is my responsibility to oversee the development and provisioning of all food for human spaceflight.*

Question: *How did you get such an interesting and demanding job?*

Ms. Kloeris: *In 1985, I was hired by Technology Incorporated (currently Wyle Labs) as a food scientist and assigned to the Space Station Food Supply and Service System (FSSS) team. The FSSS team was responsible for defining space station food system requirements and identifying areas requiring research and development. Upon completion of that assignment, I became an employee of Lockheed. Lockheed had acquired the Space Food Research and Development work, as part of the Engineering Support Contract at NASA. After a short stay with Lockheed, I was recruited by Boeing Aerospace to work on the newly* *formed Flight Equipment Processing Contract (FEPC) for the shuttle program. As the Boeing/FEPC food engineer, it was my job to bring FEPC online to produce and package shuttle food for the first FEPC supported shuttle mission, STS-26 in September 1988.*

In July 1989, NASA hired me as the subsystem manager of shuttle food. I continue to provide technical direction to two separate contracts related to shuttle food, a research and development contract and an operations contract. In January 2000, I became the subsystem manager for the International Space Food System (U.S. portion). This position involves the technical development of the food system for the ISS and for provisioning of U.S. food for the ISS crews.

Question: *What is your educational background?*

Ms. Kloeris: *In college, I majored in microbiology as an undergraduate and then got a master's degree in food science and technology. As a senior, in microbiology, I took an elective course in food microbiology. That course got me very interested in food microbiology and steered me to a graduate degree in food science and technology, which includes food microbiology. I received my bachelor of science degree in microbiology in 1978 and a master of science degree in food science and technology in December 1979—both from Texas A&M University in College Station, Texas.*

The goal of other food scientists is to increase crop yields and find new sources of protein to help feed the growing world population. According to the International Food Information Council, 10 billion people will live on Earth by the year 2050. That's about 4 billion more people than are here today. The development of meat substitutes from soybeans and other plants is an example of the work of food scientists in earlier years. Similar projects are currently underway as food scientists work to alleviate world hunger.

Food Scientists Prove Food Irradiation to Be Safe and Effective

Many food scientists spend their professional careers trying to ensure that foods are safe to eat. An early breakthrough in food safety occurred when Louis Pasteur, a French microbiologist, showed in the mid-1800s that if wine was heated to 60° Celsius (140° Fahrenheit) for thirty minutes, it did not spoil as quickly as if not treated. Pasteur also applied this principle to milk and was successful in stopping the spread of diphtheria via milk products without destroying the products' nutritional value. The process is called pasteurization. Food scientists have found that, like classical pasteurization, food irradiation kills harmful bacteria and other organisms but does not change the proteins, sugars, and other nutrients in food. Gamma rays, X-rays, and electronic beams, all of which are types of ionizing radiation, can be used to inactivate spoilage and disease-causing microorganisms without harmful changes to the food.

According to an article from the International Food Information Council entitled "Food Irradiation: A Global Food Safety Tool": "The benefits of food irradiation are that the process stops the spread of foodborne disease . . . An added advantage to this process is that food can be irradiated in its final packaging, fresh or frozen, which prevents the possibility of contamination in the distribution system, at the store or even in the home, prior to the package being opened." Food irradiation is still a controversial subject, however. Many believe that the compounds formed when food is irradiated are very dangerous to those who eat them. Food scientist and Institute of Food Technologists (IFT) irradiation expert Christine Bruhn, in a news release from the institute dated November 26, 2002, said, "Pasteurization of milk and seat belts for automobiles were controversial for a time, but we know conclusively they both save lives. The same will be true for irradiation [of food]. Those of us familiar with irradiation have an obligation to share the safety benefits of irradiated foods with the public."

Although food scientists are mainly concerned with nutrition, they also pay attention to the flavor, appearance, and texture of food. A small group of army food technologists at Natick Laboratories, a government-sponsored lab in Natick, Massachusetts, has the job of developing Meals Ready to Eat (MRE) for the one and a half million members of the United States armed forces.

Food scientists at this lab spend months and sometimes years developing foods that will remain unspoiled, nutritious, and hopefully tasty, even after several years of storage at high temperatures. There is a critical testing procedure during which the foods that have been developed are eaten and judged by a panel of military personnel. If the testers nix the food, many months of work go down the drain. Some of the foods developed by these food scientists have become commercially available. These include freeze-dried coffee, granola bars, Tang, and noodles in a cup.

FORECAST FOR THE FUTURE

According to the Career Information Center's *Agribusiness, Environment, and Natural Resources*, there are about 40,000 food scientists working in the United States. The center predicts that new jobs in the field will increase, especially in research and development and quality control.

The BLS reported that in 2000 there were about 17,500 food scientists in the United States. The discrepancy in these two reports probably reflects differences in job definitions between the two reporting agencies. The BLS predicts there will be about a 9 percent increase in this number to 19,000 by 2010. The average annual number of job openings in the field is about 720.

Michael Farr and LaVerne Ludden in *Best Jobs for the 21st Century for College Graduates* predict, however, that there will be a 20 percent growth in jobs in food science with at least 2,016 job openings each year. As the world population grows, there will be increasing demand for food scientists to improve crop yields and food preservation, and to develop new and innovative sources of food.

EDUCATION, TRAINING, AND OTHER CREDENTIALS

The Institute of Food Technologists (IFT) is the premier scientific and educational society serving the food science and technology field. Fifty-one universities with food science/technology departments or programs offer curricula and options that meet the IFT Undergraduate Education Standards for Degrees in Food Science. The IFT, through its foundation, offers scholarships to many of the students enrolled in these programs.

The programs approved by the IFT must incorporate courses in six disciplines. Students must take two general chemistry courses and at least one course in both organic chemistry and biochemistry. In the biological sciences, students must complete one general biology course and one in microbiology. The third discipline that is studied is nutrition. Students take at least one nutrition course that covers the basic concepts of general nutrition and the relationship of consumption of foods to health and well-being. Students must also take mathematics courses through calculus, one course in general physics, and one course in statistics. To complete the requirements, students must complete two courses of English, which provide the fundamentals of speaking and writing. The University of Minnesota has an IFT-approved undergraduate food science program. Refer to Table 8-1 on pages 100 and 101 for a sample curriculum. The university also lists sample job descriptions taken from actual posting announcements for food scientists with BS degrees. A few of these are:

- **Cheese Production Specialist:** Provides technical expertise for block, string, or process cheese production from milk receiving to finished product.

- **Consumer Food Assistant:** Research, development, testing, and evaluation of product ideas for advertising, promotion, and publicity. Conduct and evaluate reports on product performance. Participate in planning and execution of product commercials. Learn food styling by assisting in the preparation of product,

Table 8-1: Sample Curriculum

University of Minnesota
BS Degree in Food Service

(Courses in bold are part of the IFT minimum standards)

Freshman Year	Credits
Fall Semester	
Math 1271 Calculus 1	4
FSCN 1102 Food Safety, Risks and Technology	3
CHEM 1021 Chemical Principles 1	4
RHET 1101 Writing to Inform and Persuade	4
Spring Semester	
Math 1272 Calculus 2	4
Biology 1009 General Biology	4
CHEM 1022 Chemical Principles II	4
Arts and Humanities Lit	4

Sophomore Year	Credits
Fall Semester	
FSCN 3102 Introduction to Food Science	3
Chem 2301 Organic Chemistry 1	3
Physics I	4–5
RHET 1223 Oral Presentation in Professional Settings	3
Spring Semester	
MicB3301 Biology of Microorganisms	4
Chem 2302 Organic Chemistry II	3
Physics II	4–5
Biochemistry	3–4

Junior Year	Credits

Fall Semester

Social Sciences	4
FSCN 4111 Food Chemistry	3
FSCN 1112 Principles of Nutrition	3
RHET 3562 Technical and Professional Writing	4
BAE 4744 Engineering Principles for Biological Scientists	4

Spring Semester

FSCN4121 Food Micro and Fermentation	3
Stat 3011 Statistical Analysis	4
FSCN 4122 Lab in Micro and Fermentation	2
FSCN4332 Food Process Engineering II	3
History	4

Senior Year	Credits

Fall Semester

FSCN 4312 Food Analysis	4
FSCN 4131 Food Quality	3
Laboratory Skills	2–3

Spring Semester

FSCN 4xxx Elective with Capstone Component	3–4
Humanities/Arts	4

product-use ideas, and recipes. Develop and write label preparation instructions.

- **Flavor Chemist:** Create flavors to improve the palatability of dog and cat foods. Also identify key chemical compounds in flavors, plan and execute experiments, prepare reports, attend meetings, research literature, work with and cross train other internal team members and groups.

Most food scientists, especially those involved in research and teaching, will need either a master's degree or doctoral degree. Although only fifty-one undergraduate programs are certified by the IFT, the IFT says the graduate fellowship applicants who apply for financial aid from IFT may attend any school conducting fundamental investigation for the advancement of food science and technology.

The University of Missouri College of Agriculture, Food and Natural Resources offers both MS and Ph.D. programs in food science. The master's degree program is "designed primarily for individuals who are interested in specializing in areas of food science, food service or food distribution. The individual program is built around a core of courses in food science with supporting courses from the disciplines of chemistry, microbiology, physiology, nutrition, economics, marketing, management, and statistics. To satisfy degree requirements, candidates must:

- Complete an approved program of study.
- Prepare a thesis or, if a nonthesis option is chosen, prepare a research paper acceptable in an appropriate refereed journal based on research planned and conducted by the student in concert with an adviser.
- Pass a final oral examination over course work and research. The thesis or research paper is reviewed by each member of the final examining committee.

- Prepare at least one manuscript, acceptable for submission to a refereed journal, before approval of the M-2 (Report of the Master's Examining Committee) by the director of graduate studies.

The university's Ph.D. program in food science requires a minimum of two years beyond the master's degree. It prepares students for teaching, research, or other professional careers in food science. According to the university, "One-third of the credit earned under the plan of study is research credit, the remainder is in courses selected from food science and its supporting areas such as chemistry, microbiology, nutrition, economics, marketing, management, and statistics." It requires acceptance of a dissertation based on research proposed, performed, and defended by the student. Other requirements include taking and passing the comprehensive examination over the approved course of study and preparation of at least one manuscript acceptable for submission to a refereed journal.

INTERVIEW WITH DR. RUTH McDONALD

Dr. Ruth MacDonald is a former chairperson of the department of food science at the University of Missouri. She is now the chair of the Department of Food Science at Iowa State University. Her comments, both in an interview and in "A Word from the Chair," an article on the University of Missouri's Web site about the program at MU, are helpful for students considering a career in food science.

Question: *What is the role of a food scientist?*
Dr. MacDonald: *Food and health are intricately related, and our role as food scientists is to identify, characterize, modify, improve, and understand these relationships. Food scientists have unlimited potential to advance our knowledge of the role of foods in health and to develop foods that will provide health benefits to consumers.*

Question: *What does the Food Science Department at MU strive for?*

Dr. MacDonald: *Our goals and objectives are in parallel with the campus effort in life sciences to improve the health of Missourians and Americans through advances in food plants and animals. Food scientists will be at the heart of the interface [interaction] between identification of health benefits in foods and delivery of those benefits to consumers.*

Question: *Are students considering careers in the food sciences likely to find jobs in the future?*

Dr. MacDonald: *Regarding food science as a career, the food industry is the largest segment of the U.S. economy. Our students are readily employed by the food industry and have job offers before they graduate. It is an exciting time to be working in food science!*

In addition to supplying college scholarships, the IFT also provides the funding for the worldwide Internet distribution of a self-study learning tool designed to assist high school students in their exploration of the food industry and its career opportunities. Safeway, Inc., along with California Polytechnic University in San Luis Obispo, California, and the Arroyo Grande High School in Arroyo Grande, California, developed the program. The IFT describes the program as providing "a high-level overview of the food industry and the various career opportunities within a major food manufacturer and retailer." The contents of the program, which can be accessed from the IFT Web site, http://www.ift.org, under "Introduction to the Food Industry" are as follows:

- Lesson 1: Food Safety and Quality Assurance
- Lesson 2: Processing Food
- Lesson 3: Nutrition, Labeling, and Packaging
- Lesson 4: Integrated Resource Management

- Lesson 5: From the Plant to the Store
- Lesson 6: From the Store to the Shopper
- Lesson 7: The Customer Service Chain
- Lesson 8: Food Preparation at Home

SALARY AND BENEFITS

The Occupation Report from America's Career Infonet says that food scientists with a bachelor's degree had a median annual salary of $48,400 in 2001. The range of salaries was $28,700 to $85,300.

The Career Information Center says that salaries vary with education and experience. With a BA/BS degree, food scientists can expect to have starting salaries of about $29,000 per year. Those employed by the federal government make less with a range of salaries from $19,700 to $26,700. Experienced food scientists with Ph.D. degrees make more than $65,000 per year.

Most food scientists also receive good benefit packages with paid holidays and vacations, good health insurance, and pension plan options.

WORK ENVIRONMENT

Most food scientists work in laboratories that have pleasant working conditions and state-of-the art equipment. Their work may involve some fieldwork out-of-doors. Work hours are usually regular and rarely exceed forty hours per week. Some food technologist jobs may involve traveling to other countries, especially jobs concerned with world food supply issues.

CHAPTER 9

GENETIC ENGINEERING RESEARCH SCIENTIST

Genetic engineering (GE), one of the facets of biotechnology, is considered a relatively new profession. Some, however, believe it actually dates from 10,000 years ago—to the earliest days of agriculture. As former agriculture secretary Dan Glickman said during a speech on March 13, 1997, "Biotechnology's been around since the beginning of time. It's the caveman saving seeds of a high-yielding plant. It's Gregor Mendel, the father of genetics, cross-pollinating his garden peas."

Genetic engineering is a very controversial field. Some think that by developing the technology to manipulate genes, science has created or has the capability of creating "monsters." They disagree with Secretary Glickman's comparison of genetic engineering to the process of crossbreeding. To them, crossbreeding is a natural phenomenon while genetic engineering is an attempt to "play God."

Those who support genetic engineering are equally vocal. Marty Nemko and Paul and Sarah Edwards write in *Cool Careers for Dummies*, 2nd Edition, "A pox on those fear-mongering groups that exaggerate the danger of genetically enhanced seed. 'Frankin Food' my eye. They're essentially the same as conventionally bred seed—except that they produce crops that are healthier and/or require less pesticides."

This controversy, as well as the challenges of the work itself, makes a career as a genetic engineering research scientist particularly appealing for people who not only enjoy being on the forefront of a new technology, but who also like to be challenged to find answers to controversial questions.

Genetic engineers study farm crops and animals and develop ways of improving their quantity and quality by manipulating their genetic makeup. This is done by isolating the gene containing the DNA for the desirable trait being sought. DNA is then transferred into cells of the target plant.

FORECAST FOR THE FUTURE

Employment opportunities for both GE research scientists and assistants are excellent through at least 2006. According to the Career Information Center, "Biotechnology fields such as genetic engineering will be to the twenty-first century what microcomputers were to the twentieth century."

To realize the full potential of genetic engineering, scientists need to educate the public about it. Elizabeth Gilbert, in "Genetic Engineering of Food: For the Test Tube or Your Dinner Plate" published in the *Tufts Daily*, says that in January 2001, 60 percent of people surveyed said that they did not want genetically engineered crops introduced into food supplies. Their concerns were that the new crops were not safe. The Grocery Manufacturers of America points out,

University of Missouri GE Looks at Plant Drought Tolerance

In the early 1960s, a green revolution (a period of successful experimentation in agriculture that greatly increased productivity) occurred that doubled and tripled crop yields through the use of improved irrigation and crossbreeding. This has kept world food supplies ahead of demand for the past thirty years, according to Seth Ashley in an article in the winter 2004 issue of the University of Missouri alumni magazine. In 1996, at a World Food Summit, delegates called for a second green revolution to provide food for the world's growing population, which is projected to be 8 billion by 2025. The University of Missouri's Henry Nguyen, a researcher in molecular genetics and soybean biotechnology, is answering this call for improving crop yields by making plants more resistant to environmental stresses such as drought. Dr. Nguyen points out that some plants handle stress better than others. He says, "It's like humans. Some of us cope with stress better, and some collapse very quickly," as quoted by Seth Ashley in an article entitled "Research That Feeds the World."

It is Dr. Nguyen's goal to discover within the next four years the genetic mechanism that controls a plant's resistance to drought. Dr. Nguyen says, "We can actually look at the DNA of maize [corn] and soybeans and figure out whether a particular plant will carry the desirable genes [for drought resistance] or not. The idea is we can take something that already has a number of good characteristics and build an additional genetic system to equip it to do well under drought conditions." He goes on to say, "Drought is an important state, national, and global issue. That's why it is crucial that we learn more about the molecular basis of drought tolerance."

however, that 60 to 70 percent of all processed foods already contain genetically modified foods. Gilbert says, "The problems with genetic engineering of food [do] not lie in the science—it is in the lack of education of the people. The public does not know what genetically engineered food is, let alone what the potential risks and benefits are of such technology." Genetic engineers, or those speaking for them, will need to address public education if jobs in the field are to reach their full potential.

EDUCATION, TRAINING, AND OTHER CERTIFICATION

High school students interested in becoming genetic engineers should take biology, chemistry, physics, and advanced mathematics. Computer skills are a must for would-be genetic engineers. Attention to detail and the ability to stick with a project are personal qualities needed in this profession.

Most colleges and universities require that high school students submit scores from standardized entrance examinations as part of their entrance requirements. The two most commonly taken college entrance exams are the ACT Assessment examination and the Scholastic Aptitude Test (SAT). Students should check with colleges to which they are applying for specifics on admission examination requirements as they vary considerably from college to college.

Most genetic engineering research scientists work toward baccalaureate degrees in the biological sciences. Majors in biology, botany, or zoology with a double major or a strong minor in chemistry are common. Phill Kolodzie, author of the Web article "Construction of a Geneticist," says that it is unusual for an undergraduate student to get a degree in genetics. He believes that the undergraduate years should emphasize the basics of biology and chemistry, which will provide the foundation for later graduate work. A solid basic education is then followed by an advanced degree in microbiology, genetics, embryology, biochemistry, or other related field. Most research scientists go on to earn a Ph.D. or MD degree, although some stop with a master's degree.

Candidates for admission to graduate programs are frequently required to take admission examinations. The Graduate Record Exam (GRE) is used as one determining factor for admission to general graduate-level degree programs. It assesses a graduate school candidate's verbal, mathematical, and analytical skills. For further information on the GRE, consult the GRE Web site at http://gre.org.

The University of Arizona's graduate programs in genetics are representative of most advanced degrees in genetics across the country. Information about its graduate programs, as described on its Web site, follows.

REQUIREMENTS FOR THE M.SC. IN GENETICS

The course of study for the M.Sc. in genetics is designed to provide the student with a broad background in genetics and the cognitive sciences. To this end, all master's students are required to complete the core courses described for the Ph.D. program. The program of study will be arranged by consultation between the student and his or her major professor as early in the first semester as possible.

A master's degree may be obtained by satisfactory completion of either of the plans outlined below. The executive committee of the graduate program in genetics must approve the student's choice of plan.

Plan A: The thesis MS degree requires satisfactory completion of a minimum of 22 units of course work (15 units of these 22 must be graded A, B, etc.) and an original research project to be submitted in proper written form to the graduate college and defended orally before a three-member committee.

Plan B: A nonthesis MS degree in the graduate program in genetics requires the satisfactory completion of 30 units (15 of these 30 units must be graded A, B, etc.) of graduate courses under the guidance of the major adviser. When a student has completed all course work for the nonthesis MS degree, a committee will be assigned to examine the candidate orally.

The oral examination for students under Plan B will emphasize course work in the major area of study; for students under Plan A, the oral examination will consist of the defense of the thesis.

PH.D. PROGRAM IN GENETICS

The following is a summary of some of the general requirements for all Ph.D. degrees at the University of Arizona. Students are responsible for determining that their programs meet all the current requirements set by the graduate college.

The minimum number of units required by the graduate college for the Ph.D. is 63 units after the bachelor's degree. Of these, 36 units of coursework, plus 18 units of dissertation for a total of 54 units must be in the major in the genetics program. Students must have a minor consisting of at least 9 units of course work. All required courses must be graduate-level courses, numbered 500 or above. At least one-half of the graduate credits must be in courses in which regular grades (A, B, etc.) are earned.

Units for the minor vary according to the requirements of the minor department, usually requiring 9 to 15 units. A maximum of 6 units of 400-level courses may be used in the minor area with approval. These courses may be used to satisfy the total number of units but will not receive graduate credit and will not be calculated in the graduate GPA.

All Ph.D. students majoring in genetics or students from other programs minoring in genetics are required to take the following core courses:

a. GEN 545, Concepts in Genetic Analysis (3 credits) or GEN 627, Advanced Genetics (4 credits)
b. GEN 520, History of Genetics (1 credit)
c. GEN 568, Nucleic Acids (4 credits)
d. GEN 670, Recent Advances in Genetics (2 credits). To be taken every semester by every student enrolled in the program.

In addition to the core, a minimum of one course from each of the three following subject areas should be taken: molecular genetics, population and evolutionary genetics, and quantitative methods. The student and his/her committee should jointly decide which courses beyond the core would be appropriate. All students are required to serve as graduate teaching assistants for at least two semesters.

A qualifying examination consisting of discussion of the student's academic background and interests, and questions to ascertain the student's level of knowledge in genetics, is administered by the executive committee to students during their first semester. It is used to advise students on their courses of study for the first year.

All first-year students complete two or three rotations in laboratories of genetics faculty with a written evaluation from the head of the laboratory. Appropriate units of credit will be earned on completion of the rotations.

After all degree requirements have been satisfied and the penultimate draft of the dissertation has been approved by the dissertation committee, the candidate must submit to an oral examination in defense of the dissertation, as well as any general questioning related to the fields of study.

SALARY AND BENEFITS

Salaries for GE research scientists depend on their level of experience and the organization for which they work. Many are employed by the federal government and have a salary range less than that found in private industry. Many GE research scientists also work and teach in universities where pay scales are lower than in industry. Starting salaries range from $24,000 to $38,000 per year. Experienced GE research scientists may earn as much as $51,000 per year. Most Ph.D. and MD genetic engineers receive a salary ranging from $51,000 to $70,000 per year.

In the Footsteps of George Washington Carver

Tuskegee University in Alabama has a long history of scientific research aimed at improving crop yields to feed a hungry world. In 1896, Booker T. Washington invited George Washington Carver to join the faculty at Tuskegee. There he gained an international reputation for his agricultural research, which resulted in the creation of 325 products from peanuts and more than 100 products from sweet potatoes. These and many other products produced from plants grown in the South improved its rural economy and improved the health of many malnourished Americans.

Following in Carver's footsteps, Dr. C. S. Prakash, professor in plant molecular genetics and director of the Center for Plant Biotechnology Research at Tuskegee, oversees research on food crops of importance to the nutritional health of developing countries. He and his research group have continued Carver's work with sweet potatoes and peanuts, enhancing the protein content of crops through genetic modification. In addition to his research interests, Dr. Prakash is a teacher and a public speaker who is frequently found at conferences dealing with world hunger. He is also on the scientific advisory board of the American Council of Science and Health and serves as a speaker on behalf of the U.S. State Department. He is a strong advocate for the need to educate the public on the benefit and safety of genetic engineering.

Research scientists usually receive a full range of benefits, including paid holidays and vacations, health insurance, and pension plan options.

WORK ENVIRONMENT

Most of the work in this area is done in the research lab. Labs are pleasant, clean, and well-lit and contain state-of-the-art equipment. Scientists work between thirty-five and forty hours per week and usually do not work nights, weekends, or holidays. It may be necessary to work longer hours during some projects. Most projects are team efforts, which is usually a positive aspect of the job. Some geneticists may do fieldwork, which requires spending time outdoors.

CHAPTER 10

NUTRITION ENTREPRENEURS AND JOURNALISTS

One of the beauties of planning a career in nutrition is that there are so many choices and opportunities within the profession. You can form your own consulting firm, start a business, develop Web sites, or write about nutrition. All of these careers have one thing in common, however: they require a solid educational background in the basics of nutrition. Also, most require additional training and/or at least a year of work experience as an entry-level dietician.

NUTRITION ENTREPRENEURS

An entrepreneur is someone who assumes the risk and management of a business. Dietitians and nutritionists who start and run their own businesses are nutrition entrepreneurs. The ADA's Nutrition Entrepreneur (NE)

Dietetic Practice Group was established "for consultants in the business of developing and delivering nutrition-related services and/or products." The mission of the group is "to help members achieve their professional and financial potential by providing tools to build and maintain a successful nutrition-related business." Nondietitian nutritionists who deliver nutrition-related services or products can also be nutrition entrepreneurs.

JOB DESCRIPTION

There is no single job description that fits all the possibilities for this group. According to the NE practice group, its members "are comprised of CEOs, business owners, consultants, writers, chefs, educators, and more. Members are typically dietitians or dietetic technicians who provide professional nutrition consultation in private practice; write books, newsletters, or magazine articles; implement nutrition programs for employees in wellness programs; design nutrition software or nutrition education tools; speak professionally on wellness and nutrition topics; and work with the media."

Jill Place is a nutrition entrepreneur. She is nutrition editor of Learning Place Online, has been a professional chef, serves as a consultant to several different organizations, and gives lectures on nutrition topics. The following highlights of an interview with Ms. Place illustrate the multifaceted interests of this nutrition entrepreneur.

Question: *What prompted your interest in becoming a dietitian?*

Ms. Place: *I was a drama major as an undergraduate. After graduation, I worked in a children's theater teaching acting during the day but had a survival job as a professional chef at night. I had always loved to cook and prided myself on fixing great-tasting, healthful foods—especially low-fat foods. I was invited by one of the patrons of the restaurant where I worked to attend* *a conference given by the Diamonds [Harvey and Marilyn], the couple who wrote the book* Fit for Life. *I was so impressed by the message the Diamonds delivered that I decided to go back to school and train as a dietitian. It took five years before I became a registered dietitian, but I finally made it.*

Question: *What jobs have you held since becoming an RD?*

Ms. Place: *After passing my registration exam, I was hired by the City of Los Angeles. I planned menus and supervised the kitchen where over 1,500 meals were prepared each day for transport to senior citizen congregate meal sites throughout the city. I then became the spokesperson for Health Valley Foods, a company that specialized in the production of fat-free, low-sodium foods.*

Attending an educational seminar led to another change in my life. I went to hear Dr. Jeffery Bland, a proponent of the concept of functional medicine. What he had to say made perfect sense to me. Since then I have started my own consulting business and am trying to incorporate the concepts of functional medicine into my practice.

Question: *Whom do you deal with in your consulting business?*

Ms. Place: *I have a variety of clients. For instance, I have several individuals with whom I work. One is a young man who is receiving chemotherapy for a lymphoma. He has had repeated episodes of leukopenia [low white blood cell count] because of his treatment. This has made him especially vulnerable to infections. With the proper diet and a very specific regimen of dietary supplements, I have been able to improve his blood count and he is doing well.*

I also work with many clients on eating modification for weight loss. I strongly believe that dieting is not the way to lose weight. I work with the concept of guided imagery, a way to reprogram the brain to see oneself differently. Using this technique and good, sound dietary advice, I have been successful in helping my clients toward their weight-loss goals.

I am also the consulting dietitian for Impact House, one of the top three inpatient drug and alcohol rehabilitation facilities in the country. This job involves most of the skills of a clinical dietitian including evaluating the nutritional needs of residents, developing special diet plans, and recommending diet changes as needed.

Question: *Do you have a special interest in any particular area of nutrition?*

Ms. Place: *Yes, dietary supplements. I became interested in supplements because they play such a big role in functional medicine. I have worked with many cancer patients and have found that using massive doses of certain dietary supplements over short treatment periods positively affects not only their length of life but their quality of life. Unfortunately, the biggest dispenser of dietary supplements is the part-time clerk at your local GMC [health food] store. My crusade is to make people understand that an expert in the use of supplements should be the one directing their use, not the sales clerk. Without knowledge of drug interactions and the potentially deadly side effects of the use of supplements, a person who self-medicates or relies on information from anyone other than a professional is at risk for making him- or herself very sick indeed.*

Forecast for the Future

The blossoming of wellness clinics, spas, and health clubs has increased the demand for nutrition experts (NEs). Recognition of the national obesity epidemic has also increased the demand for experts to advise groups and individuals on weight loss topics. In an article entitled "Food and Fitness Careers for Dietitians," Cheryl J. Baldwin reports that the weight loss industry generates more than $30 billion of business each year. The sale of "functional foods" brings in more than $18 billion per year for food manufacturers.

NEs in the fitness and weight loss industries interact with multiple clients, providing both individual and group counseling as well as guidance for corporate fitness programs. One such program was developed by dietitians at the Centre Club of Cordell Medical Center in Gurnee, Illinois. The program is call Fit for Fire and is aimed at members of the local fire department.

Food companies, large corporations, major restaurant chains, and many other organizations are looking for nutrition entrepreneur consultants to help them and those they serve to realize the health benefits of good nutrition.

EDUCATION, TRAINING, AND OTHER CERTIFICATION

Dietitians who are nutrition entrepreneurs must meet the basic educational requirements for all RDs. Each consulting job may require extensive individual study on topics related to the job. Most NEs have advanced degrees in business, management, or other related fields. Some also learn on the job.

Not all nutrition entrepreneurs are dietitians. College programs like the one offered by the Department of Nutritional Sciences at Oklahoma State University (OSU) leads to a bachelor of science degree in food and nutrition. The OSU program offers several "emphasis" areas including community nutrition, food product development, nutrition and exercise science, and foods and health journalism. Nutritionists who complete this flexible program, especially if they add elective courses in areas of interest, will have a solid background on which to develop their own businesses or consulting firms.

SALARIES AND BENEFITS

Nutrition entrepreneurs are not usually employees. They may contract with a business or an organization, supplying their services for a set fee or may charge an hourly rate. Consultants may conduct seminars, weight loss classes, or other programs attended by many individuals who pay a fixed price for the program. Joanne Larsen says that RDs who work as consultants have median salaries in the $48,000 range, one of the highest salaries for an RD. Consultants to large corporations or food companies may make considerably more. Consultants do not usually receive health insurance, pension plans, and other perks.

WORK ENVIRONMENT

The work environment will vary with the job. Consultants in private practice may have very long hours, work weekends when clients are able to attend meetings, and find that their jobs require a considerable amount of travel. Nutritionists and dietitians who elect this career path must be self-starters, able to develop and stick with complex tasks and able to cope with the unexpected. This can be a highly stressful occupation.

NUTRITION JOURNALIST/EDITOR

A nutrition journalist interviews experts and conducts research to write articles about nutrition topics. A nutrition journalist may also be a food journalist whose job incorporates reporting about foods, recipes, products, and personalities for newspapers, magazines, radio, or television. If the journalist is a staff writer for a magazine or newspaper, subject matter is usually assigned based on the focus of an upcoming edition and the writer's expertise in the topics being covered in the issue.

It is the responsibility of the journalist to test all recipes being featured in his or her article to make sure no ingredients or instruction steps have been omitted. This means that the journalist must either be a cook or able to arrange for recipes to be checked by a reliable cook in a test kitchen.

A nutrition/food editor determines the subject or focus of each edition of a magazine or each radio or TV program. The editor assigns articles to staff writers and then edits those articles, selects illustrations for the articles, and approves the way the information is presented. This requires the editor to have a thorough knowledge of food ingredients, cuisines, products, nutrition issues, food trends, and who's who in the food industry.

Marlena Spieler is a nutrition/food journalist who broadcasts and writes internationally. According to information on her Web site (http://www.marlenaspieler.com), she has more than forty cookbook titles to her credit, at least two of which have won international book awards. She also writes for several newspapers and magazines as a freelance journalist and participates in food-related broadcast programs. In a brief interview, she provided the following information:

Question: *What formal training in nutrition and journalism have you had and how did you become a nutrition/food journalist?*

Ms. Spieler: *My path into food journalism was a surprise one. I trained as an artist and went to art school. My first book was written almost accidentally, as a vehicle for my artwork when I was still in my teens, so not much planning went into this decision. At that point, my only education in cuisine or nutrition was living in the Greek countryside and learning the rural ways of tradition as it pertains to food and herbal medicine. I later became very interested in nutrition via books, especially [those by] Adele Davis.*

I still have no formal training in nutrition (nor in journalism for that matter). I make it a point to keep well read on a variety of topics and on widely differing sides to those topics, so that I can learn as much as I can and finally make my own decisions on the subject.

Question: *What words of wisdom do you have for students considering nutrition/food journalism as a career?*

Ms. Spieler: *Working in a newspaper as a member of the staff is a much more secure way of living [than doing freelance writing]. Any young person thinking about writing and communicating about food should think about doing a course in journalism and also a course in culinary arts at one of the culinary institutes.*

As a freelancer, my life is not very secure, but I do love what I do: the food, the writing stories, the performing to a crowd. And I love writing books: at last count, it's hovering somewhere in the fifty-book count, though I don't know how many are still in print— maybe three or four or more.

Question: *What do you like best about being a nutrition/food journalist?*

Ms. Spieler: *The best thing about writing about food, and sharing your stories, is that it makes people happy. And, though I blush to think about it, the truth is, it makes the world a better place. People write to me all the time to tell me this. Though I wish I were more financially secure, knowing that I'm bringing happiness and health (I believe in eating lots of fruit and vegetables, too, as well as a bit of indulgence) is very, very rewarding. Also the craft of writing is very rewarding, not just for the way it communicates but for the way it makes the writer feel when it is going really well. Delicious!*

FORECAST FOR THE FUTURE

According to the Society of Professional Journalists, there are many opportunities in journalism. The careers section of its Web site notes that journalism is "a field that is wide open, with many avenues and opportunities for careers in print journalism, broadcasting, online journalism, industry, and corporate communications and beyond."

Barbara Sims-Bell says that the employment prospects for nutrition/food journalists are good, although chances for advancement may be limited. She says that the employment opportunities for food editors are limited.

Local newspapers in most towns have at least a one-day-a-week food section and there are dozens of popular food magazines. The blossoming interest in good nutrition is spawning new nutrition columns and magazines, most of which are looking for articles by freelance writers to supplement the writing of their staff journalists.

EDUCATION, TRAINING, AND OTHER CREDENTIALS

Education leading to credentials as an RD or a DTR provide an excellent background in nutrition on which a nutrition journalist can draw. The same is true for a college degree in nutrition. Many dietitians, dietetic technicians, and nutritionists write for newspapers and magazines and are consulted for expert opinions by the broadcast media. Some even have their own newspaper or magazine nutrition columns. Others are online journalists. Almost all of the nutrition professionals mentioned in this book have written for newspapers and magazines, and many have written books. Writing and communicating with the public is an essential part of what nutrition entrepreneurs do.

If nutrition journalism is approached from the journalism standpoint, it is a good idea to follow the advice of the Society of Professional Journalists, which says on its Web site (http://spj.org/careers_journalist.asp): "We suggest that if you choose journalism as a career, you do a couple of things. First choose a college with an excellent communications program. This will allow you as much access as possible to the broader areas of communications and will allow you more contact with professionals already in the field."

"Second, after you enter the program, choose your electives carefully. You will have a core curriculum of courses that are required for a communications degree. In addition to these courses, such as writing, reporting, and ethics, as a reporter you need a broad background in a variety of subjects. You will be writing about many different things, and the more you are exposed to, the better your writing will be."

"The only exception to this would be if you absolutely plan to specialize in a specific type of reporting, such as business [or nutrition]. In that case, you should focus on electives in the area where you want to specialize. "

The Missouri School of Journalism, the world's first school of journalism, is believed by many to be the best journalism school in the United States. It not only offers several undergraduate degrees in journalism but it also has master's and Ph.D. programs for those wishing advanced training. One unique program that appeals to many is called the 4&1 Program, which allows journalism undergraduates to obtain a master's degree with only two additional semesters of study. A report entitled "The Big Payoff: Educational Attainment and Synthetic Estimates of Work-Life Earnings," published by the U.S. Census Bureau in July 2002 estimates that those with a master's degree earn approximately $10,000 more per year than do those with a bachelor's degree. The extra year in the 4&1 Program may pay big dividends.

Although there are no specific accreditation programs for nutrition/food journalists, membership in the Association of Food Journalists (AFJ) is recommended for those in the field. AFJ's primary goal, according to its Web site, is "to encourage communication among food journalists. The group also strives to foster professional standards among its members and other members of the media."

SALARY AND BENEFITS

While nutrition or food journalists may be employed by a newspaper, magazine, or broadcast organization, most work as freelance contributors. If employed, salaries range from $18,000 to $35,000 per year. Freelance writers may be paid by the article or by the word. *Bon Appetit* pays from $500 to $2,000 for an article. *Diabetic Self-Management* pays up to $700 for an article, and *Cooking Light* pays $1 per word for its articles.

Barbara Sims-Bell says that food editors are paid $39,000 to $52,000 per year or more. Journalists and editors who are employed receive varying benefit packages. Freelance writers do not receive any benefits, other than authors' copies of magazines for which they write.

WORK ENVIRONMENT

Most journalists do their writing in offices or in their homes, but they may spend a considerable amount of time in various locations interviewing people working in the field of food and nutrition. Short deadlines, the necessity to rewrite, and a considerable amount of competition make a career as a nutrition/food journalist or editor a potentially stressful one.

GLOSSARY

accredit To vouch for officially; as in an accredited college.

acuity Sharpness; keenness, as of thought.

alliance Any union or connection of interests between persons, groups, states, or corporations; similarity or relationship in characteristics, structure, etc.

appendectomy In surgery, the removal of the vermiform appendix, a small saclike extension of the large intestine.

apprenticeship On-the-job training.

calorie The amount of heat or energy required to raise the temperature of one kilogram of water one degree Celsius.

cuisine The manner of preparing food for eating; the style of cooking; cookery; or the food prepared.

culinary Relating to food or the kitchen.

didactic Intended to instruct, as in teaching.

dietetics The science and art dealing with the application of principles of nutrition to the feeding of individuals or groups.

dietician One licensed in the practice of dietetics.

domain The sphere or field of activity or influence.

externship An educational experience, frequently a hands-on experience, received away from one's "home" school.

food additive A substance added to a natural food.

formulate To express in a definite or systematic way; to reduce to a formula or express as a formula.

genetically modified food Food produced from plants whose genetic makeup has been altered.

hierarchy The arrangement in order, rank, grade, class, etc., of a group of people or things.

hypermetabolism An increase in the rate at which the body produces energy for its vital functions.

hypometabolism A decrease in the rate at which the body produces energy for its vital functions.

innovate To introduce novelty; to make change in anything established.

internship A learning experience in one's "home" university, hospital, or other facility.

kinesiology The science of human motion.

malnutrition Faulty or imperfect nutrition.

metabolism The chemical changes in living cells by which energy is produced.

microorganism An organism that is too small to be seen without a microscope.

omnivorous Eating any sort of food, especially both animal and plant foods.

protocol A set of rules or list of steps to provide guidance in a scientific study.

refereed journal A journal whose articles are accepted by a panel of experts.

theoretical Limited to or based on an idea or mental plan of the way to do something.

thesis A paper produced by a candidate for a degree or diploma.

vegetarian A person who eats no meat and sometimes no animal products (such as milk or eggs).

FOR MORE INFORMATION

PROFESSIONAL SOCIETIES AND ASSOCIATIONS

American Academy of Sports Dietitians and Nutritionists
P.O. Box 4073
East Dedham, MA 02027
(857) 719-9402
Web site: http://www.aasdn.org

American College of Sports Medicine
ACSM National Center
P.O. Box 1440
Indianapolis, IN 46206-1440
(317) 637-9200
Web site: http://www.acsm.org/Sportsmed

American Culinary Federation
10 San Bartola Drive
St. Augustine, FL 32085
(904) 824-4468
Web site: http://www.acfchefs.org

American Dietetic Association
216 West Jackson Boulevard
Suite 800
Chicago, IL 60606
(312) 899-0040
Web site: http://www.eatright.org

American Pharmaceutical Association
2215 Constitution Avenue NW
Washington, DC 20037-2985
(202) 628-4410
Web site: http://www.alphanet.org

American Society of Clinical Nutrition
9650 Rockville Pike
Bethesda, MD 20814-3998
(301) 530-7110
Web site: http://www.asns.org

American Society for Hospital Food Service Administrators
840 Lake Shore Drive
Chicago, IL 60611
(312) 280-6000

American Society of Parenteral and Enteral Nutrition
8630 Fenton Street, Suite 412
Silver Springs, MD 20910
(800) 727-4567
Web site: http://www.aspenworld.com

Association of Food Journalists
38309 Genesee Lake Road
Oconomowoc, WI 53066
(414) 965-3251
(502) 583-3783
Web site: http://afjonline.com

Institute of Food Technologists
525 West Van Buren
Suite 1000
Chicago, IL 60607
(312) 782-8424
Web site: http://www.ift.org

International Food Information
Council Foundation
1100 Connecticut Avenue NW
Suite 430
Washington, DC 20036
(202) 296-6540
Web site: http://www.ific.org

National Association of
Sports Nutrition
7710 Balboa Avenue, Suite 227B
San Diego, CA 92111
(858) 694-0317
Web site: http://www.
nasnutrition.com

EDUCATIONAL INSTITUTIONS

FOR DIETITIANS AND DIETETIC TECHNICIANS

The Commission on Accreditation for Dietetic Education (CADE) has approved more than 600 undergraduate and graduate didactic, dietetic technician, and supervised practice programs to prepare dietetics professionals. A sample listing of approved programs in each category is given here and is available on the Web site of the American Dietetics Association (http://www.eatright.org).

DIDACTIC PROGRAMS IN DIETETICS

Brigham Young University
Food Science and
  Nutrition Department
S219 ESC
P.O. Box 24620
Provo, UT 84602-4620
(801) 378-8714

Georgia State University
Department of Nutrition
Box 873
University Plaza
Atlanta, GA 30303-3083
(404) 651-1108

Idaho State University
Department of Health and
  Nutrition Sciences
Box 8109
Pocatello, ID 83209-2532
(208) 236-2352

Indiana University
Department of Applied
  Health Science
HPER 116
Bloomington, IN 47405-4801
(812) 855-3936

Montana State University
Department of Health and
  Human Development
201 Romney Gym
Bozeman, MT 59717-0336
(406) 994-6338

New York University
Department of Nutrition and
  Food Studies
35 West 4th Street
10th Floor
New York, NY 10012-1172
(212) 995-4194

North Dakota State University
Department of Food and Nutrition

College of Human Development
and Education
Box 5057
Fargo, ND 58105-5057
(701) 231-7474

Ohio University
School of Human and
 Consumer Sciences
101 Tupper Hall
Athens, OH 45701-2979
(740) 593-2874

Oregon State University
Nutrition and Food Management
 Dietetic Program
148 Milam Hall
Corvalis, OR 97331-5103
(541) 737-6914

**The Pennsylvania
 State University**
Nutrition Department
College of Health and
 Human Development
University Park, PA 16802-6500
(814) 863-6103

Texas Woman's University
Department of Nutrition
 and Dietetics
Box 298600
TWU Station 425888
Denton, TX 76204-5888

University of Alabama
Department of Human Nutrition
 and Hospitality Management
Box 870158
Tuscaloosa, AL 35487-0158
(205) 348-4710

University of Arizona
Department of
 Nutritional Sciences

Tucson, AZ 85721
(520) 621-1619

University of California, Berkeley
Department of
 Nutritional Sciences
119 Morgan Hall
Berkeley, CA 94720-3104
(510) 642-4090

University of Delaware
Department of Nutrition
 and Dietetics
234 Alison Hall
Newark, DE 19716-3301
(302) 831-8765

University of Florida
Food Science and Human
Nutrition Department
359 FSB
Gainesville, FL 32611
(352) 392-1991

University of Illinois
Department of Food Science
 and Human Nutrition
345 Bevier Hall
905 S. Goodwin Avenue
Urbana, IL 61801
(217) 244-2884

University of Maine
Department of Food Science
 and Human Nutrition
5749 Merrill Hall
Room 27
Orono, ME 04469-5749
(207) 581-3111

University of Maryland
Department of Nutrition
 and Food Science
College Park, MD 20742-7521
(301) 405-4531

University of Massachusetts
Department of Nutrition
Box 31420
Chenoweth Laboratory
Amherst, MA 01003-1420
(413) 545-0740

University of Minnesota
Department of Food Science
 and Nutrition
1334 Eckles Avenue
St. Paul, MN 55108-6099
(612) 624-3255

**University of
 Southern Mississippi**
School of Home Economics
Box 3053
Hattiesburg, MS 39406-5035
(601) 266-4679

University of Nevada, Reno
Department of Nutrition
Mail Stop 142
Reno, NV 89557-0132
(702) 784-6449

**University of North Carolina,
 Chapel Hill**
Department of Nutrition
McGavran-Greenberg Hall,
 CB#7400
Chapel Hill, NC 27599-7400
(919) 966-7216

University of Puerto Rico
School of Home Economics
Box 23347, UPR Station
Rio Piedras Campus
San Juan, PR 00931-3347
(787) 764-0000

University of Rhode Island
Department of Food Science
 and Nutrition

17 Woodward Hall
Kingston, RI 02881-0804
(401) 874-4017

University of Tennessee
College of Human Ecology
Department of Nutrition
Room 229
1215 Cumberland Avenue
Knoxville, TN 37996-1900
(423) 974-6244

**University of
 Wisconsin, Madison**
Department of
 Nutritional Sciences
1415 Linden Drive
Madison, WI 53706-1517
(608) 262-5860

University of Wyoming
Department of Family and
 Consumer Sciences
Laramie, WY 82071-3354
(307) 766-3379

Virginia State University
Department of Human Ecology
Box 9211
Petersburg, VA 23806
(804) 524-5502

COORDINATED
UNDERGRADUATE PROGRAMS

**Edinboro University
 of Pennsylvania**
Department of Biology
 and Health Services
Edinboro, PA 16444
(814) 732-2458

Framingham State College
Department of Family
 and Consumer Sciences

100 State Street
Framingham, MA 01701-9101
(508) 626-4754

Mount Mary College
Department of Dietetics
2900 North Menomonee
  River Parkway
Milwaukee, WI 53222-4597
(414) 256-1224

Purdue University
Department of Food
  and Nutrition
1264 Stone Hall
West Lafayette, IN 47907-1264
(765) 494-8236

The University of Connecticut
School of Allied Health
353 Mansfield Road U101
Storrs, CT 06269-2101
(860) 486-0016

University of Idaho
School of Family and
  Consumer Sciences
College of Agriculture
Moscow, ID 83844-3183
(208) 885-6026

**University of Missouri,
  Columbia**
Dietetic Education
318 Clark Hall
Columbia, MO 65211
(573) 884-4137

**University of Medicine and
  Dentistry of New Jersey**
School of Health
  Related Professions
63 Bergen Street
Newark, NJ 07107-3001
(973) 972-6245

Utah State University
Department of Nutrition
  and Food Sciences
Logan, UT 84322-8700
(801) 797-2105

**Washington State
  University**
FSHN Building 106F
P.O. Box 646376
Pullman, WA 99164-6376
(509) 335-1395

Wayne State University
Department of Nutrition
  and Food Science
3009 Science Hall
Detroit, MI 48202
(313) 577-2500

DIETETIC TECHNICIAN PROGRAMS

Ball State University
Department of Family and
  Consumer Sciences
150 Applied Technology
Muncie, IN 47306
(765) 285-2255

Briarwood College
2279 Mount Vernon Road
Southington, CT 06489
(860) 628-4751

Camden County College
P.O. Box 200
Blackwood, NJ 08012
(609) 227-7200

Central Arizona College
8470 N. Overfield Road
Coolidge, AZ 85228
(520) 426-4497

El Paso Community College
100 West Rio Grande Avenue
El Paso, TX 79902
(915) 831-4470

Lima Technical College
4240 Campus Drive
Lima, OH 45804-3597
(419) 995-8328

Nebraska Methodist College
Metropolitan Community
Consortium
8501 W. Dodge Road
Omaha, NE a68114
(402) 354-8875

Palm Beach Community College
Dietetic Technician Program
4200 Congress Avenue

Mail Station 32
Lake Worth, FL 33461-4796
(561) 439-8314

Portland Community College
12000 S.W. 49th
P.O. Box 19000
Portland, OR 97280-0990
(503) 977-4029

Spokane Community College
N. 1810 Greene Street
MS 2090
Spokane, WA 99207-5399
(509) 533-7314

Tidewater Community College
1700 College Crescent
Virginia Beach, VA 23456
(757) 822-7336

FOR FOOD SCIENTISTS/TECHNOLOGISTS

The Institute of Food Technologists offers a directory of universities which meet the IFT Undergraduate Education Standard for Degrees in Food Science. A sampling of the schools with these programs is listed. A complete list of the fifty-one programs approved by IFT is available on its Web site (http://www.ift.org).

Alabama A&M University
Department of Food and
  Animal Sciences
P.O. Box 1628
Normal, AL 35762
(256) 858-4166

Cornell University
Department of Food Science
114 Stocking Hall
Ithaca, NY 14853-7201
(607) 254-4868

Rutgers University
Cook College Department of
  Food Science
65 Dudley Road
New Brunswick, NJ 08901-8520
(732) 932-9611

Tuskegee University
Department of Food
  and Nutritional Sciences
204 T. M. Campbell Hall
Tuskegee, AL 36088
(334) 727-8323

University of Idaho
Department of Food Science
  and Technology
P.O. Box 442201
2222 West 6th Street
Moscow, ID 83844-2201
(208) 885-7081

University of Missouri, Columbia
College of Agriculture, Food
  and Natural Resources
122 Eckles Hall
256 WC Stringer Wing
Columbia, MO 65211-5140
(573) 882-4113

FOR THE CULINARY ARTS

There are more than 3,000 cooking schools and culinary institutes in the United States. The Culinary Schools Directory at http://www. culinary-schools.org offers links to many other directories and provides a list of the culinary institutes and schools that the site's editors believe to be the top culinary schools in the country. Also, twelve schools offering the Le Cordon Bleu Program are listed on the College Search Engine at http://www.collegesearchengine.org/culinary/le-cordon-bleu. html. A sample listing of professional cooking schools follows.

Atlantic Community College Academy of Culinary Arts
Mays Landing, NJ 08330

California Culinary Academy
625 Polk Street
San Francisco, CA 94102

Clark College Culinary Arts Department
1800 East McLoughlin Boulevard
Vancouver, WA 98663

The Culinary Institute of America
433 Albany Post Road
Hyde Park, NY 12538

The Culinary School of Kendall College
2408 Orrington Avenue
Evanston, IL 60201

The French Culinary Institute
462 Broadway
New York, NY 10013

Johnson and Wales University
Culinary Arts Division
1 Washington Avenue
Providence, RI 02905

The Natural Gourmet Cooking School/The Natural Gourmet Institute of Food and Health
48 West 21st Street, 2nd floor
New York, NY 10010

New England Culinary Institute
250 Main Street
Montpelier, VT 05602

New York Restaurant School
27 West 34th Street
New York, NY 10001

FOR PHARMACISTS

The Official World List of Pharmacy Schools (WLPS) is published by the International Pharmaceutical Federation (IPF) in collaboration with the International Pharmaceutical Students Federation (IPSF). The directory contains the postal address and other contact information for more than 900 schools of pharmacy worldwide. It may be accessed at http://www.fip.org/education. A sample listing of schools of pharmacy follows:

Oregon State University
College of Pharmacy
203 Pharmacy Building
Corvalis, OR 97331-3507
(541) 737-3424

University of Maryland
School of Pharmacy
20 North Pine Street
Baltimore, MD 21201-1180
(410) 706-7651

**St. Louis College
 of Pharmacy**
4588 Parkview Place
St. Louis, MO 63110-1088
(314) 367-8700

University of Tennessee
College of Pharmacy
847 Monroe Avenue, Suite 226
Memphis, TN 38163
(901) 448-6036

University of Kansas
School of Pharmacy
2056 Malott Hall
Lawrence, KA 66045-2500
(785) 864-3591

University of Texas at Austin
College of Pharmacy
2409 University Avenue
Austin, TX 78712-1074
(512) 471-3718

INTERNSHIPS

The following are institutions that offer ADA-approved dietetic internships. For a more complete listing, visit the ADA's Web site (http://www.eatright.org/public/7782-13285.cfm).

ARAMARIC Corporation
Mid-Atlantic Dietetic Internship
41 Pebble Ridge Road
Warrington, PA 18976
Contact: Patricia Richards
(800) 466-4272 ext.238
e-mail: richards.pat@
 aramaric.com

St. Mary's Hospital
Mayo Clinic
1216 2nd Street SW
Rochester, MN 55902-1906
Contact: Jeanne Grant
(507) 255-5617
e-mail: grant.jeanne
 @mayo.edu

Texas Department of Health
Bureau of Nutrition Science
1100 West 49th Street
Austin, TX 78756
Contact: Sherry Clark
(512) 458-7111
e-mail: sherry.clark@tdh.state.tx.us

University of Maine
Department of Food Science and Human Nutrition
5735 Hitchner Hall, Room 113
Orono, ME 04469-5735
Contact: Adrienne White
(207) 581-3134
e-mail: aawhite@umenfa.maine.edu

U.S. Military Dietetics Internship Consortium
Walter Reed Army Medical Center
Nutrition Care Directorate
2900 Georgia Avenue NW
Washington, DC 20307-5001
Contact: Deborah De Pastina
(202) 782-0387
e-mail: deborah.depastina@na.amedd.arm.md

VA San Diego Healthcare System
Dietetics and Clinical Nutrition Service (120)
3350 LaJolla Village Drive
San Diego, CA 92161-0002
Contact: Teresa Bush-Zurn
(858) 552-8505
e-mail: teresa.bush-zurn@med.va.gov

Washington State University
310 North Riverpoint Boulevard
P.O. Box 1495
Spokane, WA 99210-1495
Contact: Janet K Beary
(509) 358-7562
e-mail: beary@wsu.edu

RESIDENCIES

The American College of Clinical Pharmacy has compiled a directory that lists 353 programs that offer residency training programs in pharmacy, 80 programs which offer fellowships, and 3 programs that offer a residency combined with a fellowship. The directory can be accessed from the organization's Web site (http://www.accp.org).

SCHOLARSHIPS

IN DIETETICS

The American Dietetic Association Foundation awards scholarships to students in accredited dietetic programs. The scholarship awards are generally for ADA student members enrolled in their junior or senior years in a baccalaureate program or a coordinated program in dietetics. Scholarships are also awarded in the second year of a dietetic

Texas Department of Health
Bureau of Nutrition Science
1100 West 49th Street
Austin, TX 78756
Contact: Sherry Clark
(512) 458-7111
e-mail: sherry.clark@tdh.state.tx.us

University of Maine
Department of Food Science and Human Nutrition
5735 Hitchner Hall, Room 113
Orono, ME 04469-5735
Contact: Adrienne White
(207) 581-3134
e-mail: aawhite@umenfa.maine.edu

U.S. Military Dietetics Internship Consortium
Walter Reed Army Medical Center
Nutrition Care Directorate
2900 Georgia Avenue NW
Washington, DC 20307-5001
Contact: Deborah De Pastina
(202) 782-0387
e-mail: deborah.depastina@na.amedd.arm.md

VA San Diego Healthcare System
Dietetics and Clinical Nutrition Service (120)
3350 LaJolla Village Drive
San Diego, CA 92161-0002
Contact: Teresa Bush-Zurn
(858) 552-8505
e-mail: teresa.bush-zurn@med.va.gov

Washington State University
310 North Riverpoint Boulevard
P.O. Box 1495
Spokane, WA 99210-1495
Contact: Janet K Beary
(509) 358-7562
e-mail: beary@wsu.edu

RESIDENCIES

The American College of Clinical Pharmacy has compiled a directory that lists 353 programs that offer residency training programs in pharmacy, 80 programs which offer fellowships, and 3 programs that offer a residency combined with a fellowship. The directory can be accessed from the organization's Web site (http://www.accp.org).

SCHOLARSHIPS

IN DIETETICS

The American Dietetic Association Foundation awards scholarships to students in accredited dietetic programs. The scholarship awards are generally for ADA student members enrolled in their junior or senior years in a baccalaureate program or a coordinated program in dietetics. Scholarships are also awarded in the second year of a dietetic technician program. Application forms and more information about scholarships are available from the ADA accreditation and student operation staff at (800) 877-1600 or at education@eatright.org.

The American Dietetic Association Foundation has also released the second edition of the ADAF Directory of Resources for International Food, Nutrition, and Dietetics Professionals. This reference is for those seeking funding for professional study, work experience, or research in their home countries or abroad. It lists more than 100 groups offering financial assistance and features educational organizations, loan programs, and Internet resources. A free copy may be obtained by e-mail at epuga@eatright.org.

In the Culinary Arts

The National Restaurant Association Educational Foundation awarded $1.4 million in scholarships in 2003 and 2004. The foundation provides four types of scholarships: academic scholarships for high school students interested in culinary arts, ProStart national certificates of achievement scholarships, academic scholarships for undergraduate college students, and professional development scholarships for educators in the culinary arts. For more information about these contact:

Scholarships and Mentoring Initiative
National Restaurant Association Education Foundation
175 West Jackson Boulevard, Suite 1500
Chicago, IL 60604-2814
(800) 765-2122 ext. 733 or (312) 717-1010
e-mail: scholars@foodtrain.org

Other scholarships available in the hospitality industry include:
- The American Academy of Chefs Caine des Rotisseurs Scholarship. Twenty $1,000 scholarships are usually awarded each year to students in two- and four-year culinary programs. Information on these two scholarship programs may be accessed from the American Culinary Foundation's Web site (http://www.acfchefs. org/educate/eduschlr.html).
- Hospitality Sales and Marketing Association International (HSMAI) offers scholarships for those in hospitality fields. Information is available at http://www.hsmai.org.
- The American Institute of Wine and Food has information about scholarships at http://www.aiwf.org.
- The James Beard Foundation offers culinary arts scholarships to study in the United States or abroad. Information is available at http://www.jamesbeard.org/Scholarships/friends_list.shtml.

In the Food Industry

The Institute of Food Technologists administers scholarships to outstanding undergraduate and graduate students. For information on these scholarships and fellowships, contact the IFT Scholarship Department at (312) 782-8424 or e-mail Patti Pagliuco at pgpagliuco@ift.org.

Licensure, Registration, and Certification

**Dietitians and
  Dietetic Technicians**
Commission on
  Dietetic Registration
1205 Riverside Plaza, Suite 2000
Chicago, IL 60606-6995
(312) 899-0040 ext. 5500
Web site: http://www.cdrnet.org

Sports Nutrition
The Academy of Sports
  Dietitians and Nutritionists
P.O. Box 4073
East Dedham, MA 02027
(857) 719-9402
Web site: http://www.aasdn.org

Nutrition Support for Dietitians
National Board of Nutrition
  Support Certification, Inc.
  (NBNSC)
Web site: http://www.
  nutritioncertify.org.

Pharmacists
North American Pharmacy
Licensing Examination
  (NAPLEX)
Carmen A. Catizone

National Association of
  Boards of Pharmacy
700 Busse Highway
Parkridge, IL 60608
(847) 698-6227
Web site: http://www.nabp.net/
  index

Nutrition Support Pharmacist
The Board of
  Pharmacy Specialties
Web site: http://www.bpsweb.org.

Culinary Arts
The American Culinary
  Federation(ACFCP)
Web site: http://www.acfchefs.org

Food Service Management (FSM)
The National Restaurant
Association Educational
  Foundation
175 West Jackson Boulevard
Suite 1500
Chicago, IL 60604-2814
ATTN: Course and Exam
Administration Department
(312) 715-1010, ext. 703
Web site: http://www.nraef.org

FOR FURTHER READING

American Dietetic Association. *2002 Dietetics Compensation and Benefit Survey*. Chicago, IL: American Dietetic Association, 2003.

Bender, David, and Arnold Bender. *Nutrition: A Reference Handbook*. New York: Oxford University Press, 1997.

Bureau of Labor Statistics. *U.S. Department of Labor. Occupational Outlook Handbook*. New York: McGraw Hill/Contemporary Books, 2002.

Camenson, Blythe. *Careers for Health Nuts and Others Who Like to Stay Fit* (Careers for You Series). New York: McGraw-Hill/Contemporary Books, 1996.

College Blue Book, Degrees Offered by College and Subject. New York: Macmillan Publishing, 2000.

Heitzmann, William. *Opportunities in Sports Medicine Careers*. New York: McGraw-Hill/Contemporary Books, 1992.

Jennigan, Ann K., and Dorothea Turner. *Nutrition in Long Term Care Facilities: A Handbook for Dietitians*. Chicago: American Dietetics Association, 2002.

Payne-Palacio, June, and Monica Theis. *West and Wood Introduction to Food Service*. New York: Prentice Hall, 2001.

Ruhlman, Michael. *The Making of a Chef: Mastering Heat at the Culinary Institute of America*. New York: Henry Hold and Co. LLC, 1997,

Rudman, Jack. *Registration Exam for Dietitians* (Red Admission Test Series). Syosset, NY: National Learning Company. 1999.

BIBLIOGRAPHY

AgBioWorld.org. "Dr. Channapatna S. Prakash, Professor, Plant Molecular Genetics, Tuskegee University. Alabama, USA." Retrieved December 2003 (http://www.agbioworld.org/biotechinfo/ articles/prakash/prakashart/prakash_bio.html).

Ashley, Seth. "Research That Feeds the World." *Mizzou*, Winter 2004.

Baldwin, Cheryl. "Food and Fitness Careers for Dietitians." *Journal of the American Dietetics Association*, November 2002.

Caldwell, Carol. *Opportunities in Nutrition Careers*. Lincolnwood, IL: VGM Career Horizons, 2000.

Career Information Center, Seventh ed. *Volume 1: Agribusiness, Environment, and Natural Resources*. New York: Macmillan Reference USA, 1999.

Career Information Center, Seventh ed. *Volume 5: Consumer, Homemaker, Personal Services*. New York: Macmillan Reference USA, 1999.

Career Information Center, Seventh ed. *Volume 6: Engineering, Science and Technology*. New York: Macmillan Reference USA, 1999.

Career Information Center, Seventh ed. *Volume 8: Hospitality and Recreation*. New York: Macmillan Reference USA, 1999.

Carlin, Joseph. "Pleasures of the Table: Eating and Drinking in the Early Republic." *Nutrition Today*, March-April 1998.

CookingSchools.com. "Interview with Chef Alex Askew, Black Culinarian Alliance." Retrieved December 2003 (http://cookingschools.com/ interviews/alex-askew).

CookingSchools.com. "Interview with Chef Daniel Boulud." Retrieved December 2003 (http://www.cookingschools.com/interviews/daniel-boulud).

CookingSchools.com. "Interview with Joan Carter, Dietitian and Nutritionist." Retrieved December 2003 (http://www.cookingschools.com/interviews/joan-carter).

CookingSchools.com. "Interview with Joe LaVilla." Retrieved December 2003 (http://www. cookingschools.com/articles/career-planning).

Dickerson, Roland, and Rex Brown. "Education and Training in Nutrition Support Pharmacy Practice." *Nutrition*, 19:693-697, 2003.

Donovan, Mary. *Careers for Gourmets and Others Who Relish Food.* Lincolnwood, IL: NTC Publishing, 1993.

Duke University Web site. "A Team Approach to Nutrition Support." Retrieved December 2003 (http://surgery.mc.duke.edu/nutrition/secure/team_approach.html).

Farr, Michael, and LaVerne Ludden. *Best Jobs for the 21st Century for College Graduates.* Indianapolis, IN: Jist Works, Inc., 2000.

Gilbert, Elizabeth. "Genetic Engineering of Food: For the Test Tube or Your Dinner Plate?" *The Tufts Daily*, April 3, 2001. Retrieved December 2003 (http://www.nutrition.tufts.edu/news/matters/2001-04-03.html).

Hasenauer, Heike. "Cultivating Cooks." Retrieved December 2003 (http://www.army.mil/soldiers/apr97/text/cookst.html).

Heaf, David. "Becoming a Genetic Engineer." Ifgene.org. Retrieved January 2004 (http://www.anth.org/ifgene/gecareer.htm).

Hoffman, Randy. "Learning to Serve, Serving to Learn: An Introduction to Cooking Schools and Culinary Institutes." CookingSchools.com, October 8, 2003. Retrieved December 2003 (http://www.cookingschools.com/introduction).

HunterCollege.edu. "Laws that Regulate Dietitian/ Nutritionists" Retrieved January 2004 (http://www. hunter.cuny.edu/schoolhp/phn/regulations.htm).

IFT.org. "Introduction to the Food Industry." Retrieved December 2003 (http://www.ift.org/cms/?pid = 1000411).

IFT.org. "Scientific facts: Uphill Battle Vs. Irradiation Misinformation" Retrieved January 2004 (http://www. ift.org/cms/?pid = 1000489).

Keeler, Janet. "Fueling the Olympic Fire." *St. Petersburg Times*, September 13, 2000. Retrieved December 2003 (http://www.foodandsport.com/olympicstory1.htm).

Kloeris, Vicki. "My Journals." NASA.gov. Retrieved December 2003 (http:// quest.arc.nasa.gov/people/ bios/space/kloeris.html).

Krannich, Ronald, and C. Rae Krannich. *The Best Jobs for the 21st Century*. Third ed. Manassas Park, VA: Impact Publications, 1998.

Larsen, Joanne. "Ask the Dietitian: Careers in Nutrition and Dietetics." Dietician.com. Retrieved December 2003 (http://www.dietitian.com/rds.html).

Lyons, Dianne. *Planning Your Career in Alternative Medicine*. Garden City Park, NY: Avery Publishing Group, 1997.

Penn State Web site. "Dietetic Programs Through Distance Education-Health Care Emphasis (Dietetic Technician Program)." Retrieved December 2003 (http://www.hrrm. psu.edu/dpde/dtmore.htm).

Ruppaport, Karen, ed. *The Directory of Schools for Alternative and Complementary Health Care*. Phoenix, AZ: Oryx Press, 1998.

Sims-Bell, Barbara. *Career Opportunities in the Food and Beverage Industry*. New York: Facts on File, Inc., 1994.

INDEX

ABOUT THE AUTHOR

Linda Bickerstaff, MD, is a retired surgeon who writes from her home in Ponca City, Oklahoma.